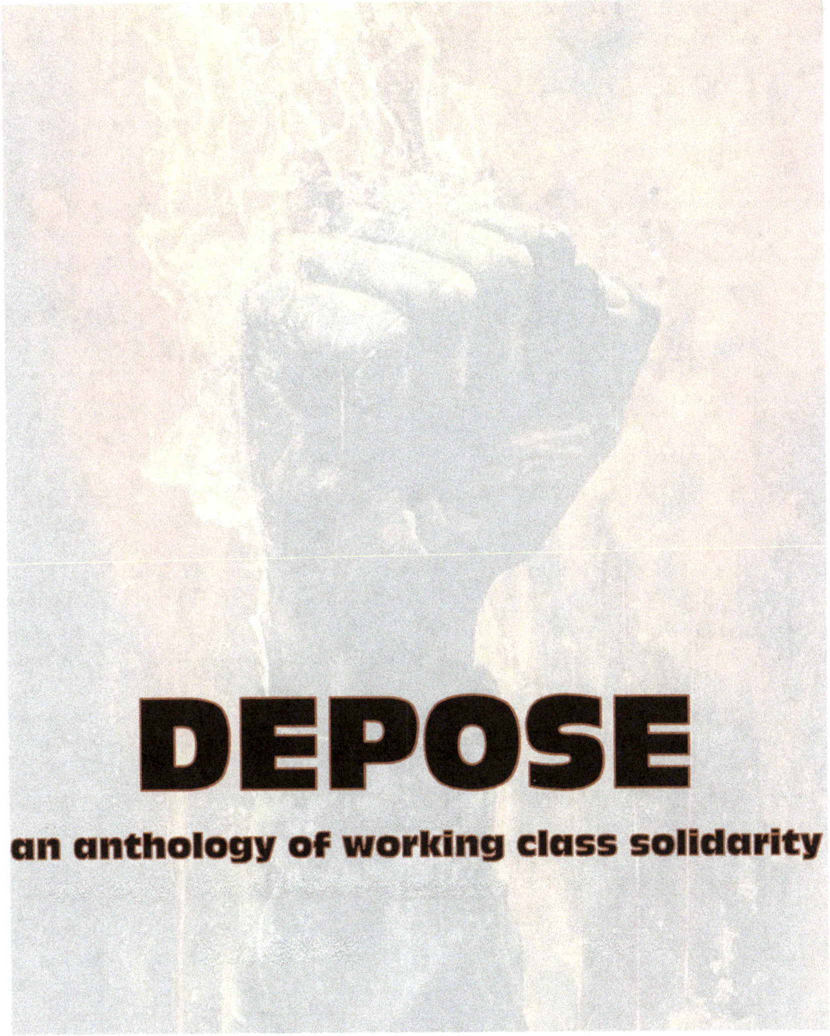

DEPOSE

an anthology of working class solidarity

Selection/Edition by Mark Lipman

VAGABOND
VENICE, CA/BOSTON/MILAN

FAIR USE NOTICE

editor@vagabondbooks.net

Published by VAGABOND
Mark Lipman, editor

VAGABOND

*The only way we'll get freedom for ourselves
is to identify ourselves with every oppressed people in the world.*

~ Malcolm X

TABLE OF CONTENTS

DEPOSE

an anthology of working class solidarity

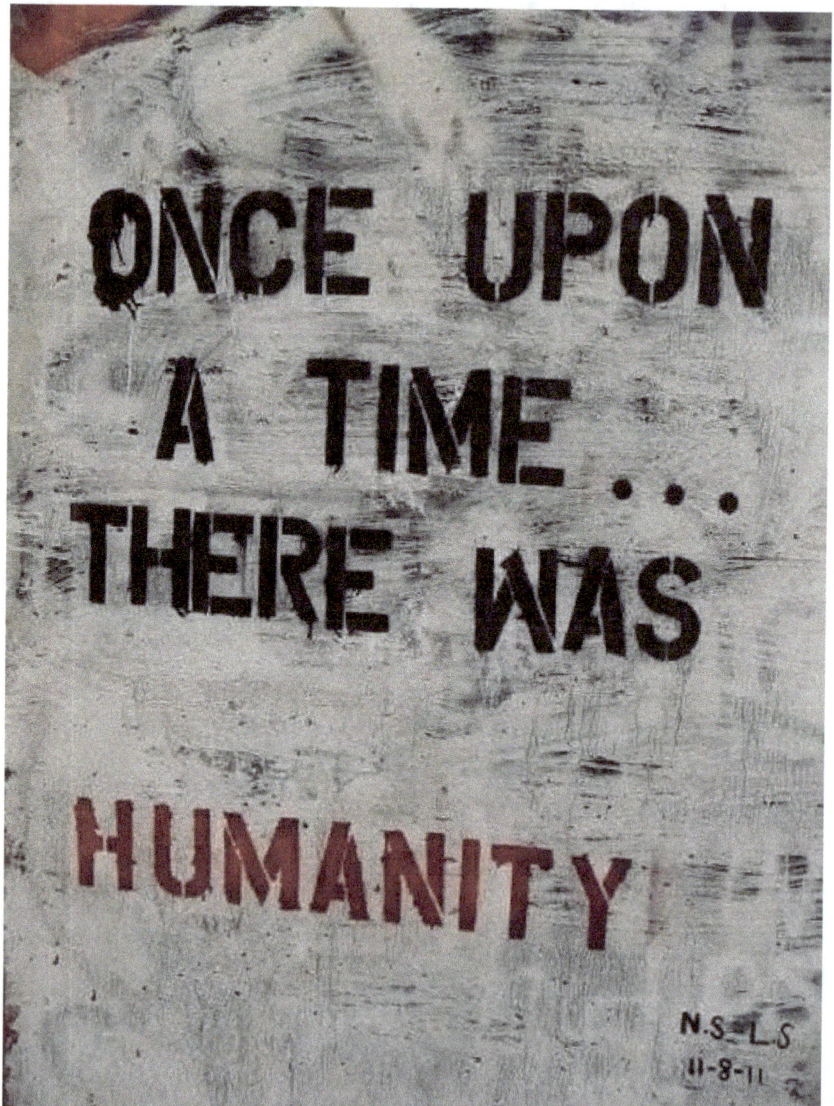
ONCE UPON
A TIME ...
THERE WAS
HUMANITY
N.S. L.S
11-8-11

... for all those who've been silenced.

Introduction

In these Crazy Times

There is no choice we have over when we were born, only for what we do in the times in which we live... and these crazy times of divisiveness, false justifications and mirrors, of war crimes and genocide, of premeditated cruelty and fascism, call for action, call for a new vision, call for the poets to raise their voices and speak up about what's really going on in this world that has gone right off the rails and over the edge, straight into insanity, when we are programmed to live backwards and to the opposite of anything that is in harmony with nature or the way we could easily be, if we just worked collectively... for the common good.

The choices we make right now, in these crazy and dangerous times, will determine the fate for not just ourselves, but for every possible future every living thing on this planet could have... forever.

Right now, we are on course for not just mass human extinction, through wars, genocide, austerity and pure carelessness, as those with everything squeeze us into concentration camps and mass graves, but we're taking the whole planet with us in the process, destroying our entire eco-system and endangering the lives of every species on the planet. What we are doing right now as nations and a people, is a crime so great that it defies the language to name.

For over two years we have watched a genocide, supported by both factions of the capitalist political duopoly, take this world onto the brink of all-out war and annihilation. What they have done to Gaza they will gladly do to any of us too.

We have watched how the collapse of morality and the undermining of our democratic processes, by the party that only gives lip service to our great suffering, gave rise to the outright fascists with their white nationalist, racist and misogynistic agendas, who have sent armed, masked thugs into our communities to tear the fabric of this nation and its people apart.

To love a country, or any place really, you must first love its people, for that is what a country is, a massive gathering of people in every shade of color, for it's our differences and diversity that make us strong, and somewhere along the line our government has forgotten that.

Truly, this is a moment of great danger... but it's also one of transformation.

It's said that change only happens when your back is up against the wall... and here we are, born into a moment in time that is on the brink of extinction, and the best we might only be able to do at this point is mitigate the damage.

If there's any hope to turn all this around, it will only come through our class solidarity... of each receiving what they need, while doing what they can to make a better world than the one that was left to them. It's our working class diversity that gives us our strength... we each have something to contribute... and we are the many... nothing is beyond our reach.

As poets, as writers, our contribution is our empathy... of feeling these issues so deeply that we put the entirety of our thought and the years of our lives to put all this into words, so that those with other abilities can take those ideas and make them a reality... for anything we can imagine, we can make real.

The evolution of our times is now upon us and collectively this is our time to act, to stand up and say enough... that it's time to throw the old ways out and go in a new direction... one where we place our energy into healing this planet and caring for all, of having space for everyone... for this is not a competition.

We have the right to rewrite the rules, so that they favor the many... for when we all win, we all win.

These are some of the thoughts that enter my head as I put this collection together, bringing poets from around the world together to have this much needed conversation of how we depose of a corrupted system of greed that benefits only a few, while lifting up the many in solidarity with our working class sisters and brothers.

~ Mark Lipman, editor

HANDS IN THE FIRE

The weight of the brush, the steel of the pen
Calloused hands carve truth into the stone
A mountain of ethics un-movable by men
They tell us to make, but not to take
to build, but never own
To fear but never fight

Sweat runs down on the canvas
Ink bleeds through the cracks
We are ghosts in their walls
They feast on the work of our hands
While we starve on the dust of their power

They set the price, break the backs
They call it passion, we call it survival
But survival doesn't ask for suffering
and passion doesn't beg for scraps

We see each other
In the dim glow of factory lights
As we walk through asbestos clouds
In the cold rooms where art is made, not sold
They want us alone, want us afraid
But we are many, and they are old

Hands in the fire
Voices in the storm
No more waiting, no more chains.
If we build their world, we can tear it down,
and rise from the ashes they left us in.

SHIT KICKERS

They came in wearing steel-toed boots
Hands blackened with oil and powder
Dark rouge adorned their lips and cheeks
Laughter swallowed by the roar of the line
Where rivets sparked like dying stars
and the war moved beneath
Their petite fingers

Their names were stitched in silence
Some of their men even had them tattooed
They were stitched into canvas, into steel
Into the bones of ships that never knew them
They were sent screaming
Into the salted dark sea
Bearing the weight of hands unshaken

In the dust-choked air of the factories
They built the coffins
Of their own: brothers, lovers, sons
Not yet buried
While telegrams whispered through doorways
Bodies vanished across the sea
Women were made stronger
Because they had to be

At night, they dreamed of metal kisses
Of heat pressing hugs into their skin
Of the weight of wrenches in their grip
And in the empty houses they left behind
The clocks never stopped ticking

The war would end without them
But the ghosts of their work remained
Silent, rusted, waiting in fields and harbors
Nose-diving planes
Just another memory of hands
That held the world together
Our hair stays curled, lashes flutter
In remembrance
These shit kickers were our grandmothers

A native of Detroit, **Lisa Bennington-Love** is a poet who uses her experiences to bring awareness to abuse, addiction, and domestic violence. She tempers her work with a dark, wry, sense of humor. Lisa has four books of poetry and has even garnered praise from punk icon, Exene Cervenka. When not writing, Lisa is currently earning an MFA in Creative Writing. She enjoys collage art, photography, and volunteers at a homeless charity regularly.

NEXT

pack it all up
we're on to the next place
the last one was burned down
for money

what else?

tradition – it's how it's always been
& how it's always going to be
it's all we know

what do we know?

at this knew place
where the birds come to pray
standing on elms
looking down

are they next or us?

we're just like the disease
aren't we?
parasites onto ourselves
will the leaves ever

reach the ground again?

& we'll still say
we're in love with it all
then wonder what we can do
we stand in shock
surprised
but not enough to stop
the leaves have teeth
shaped like saws
their veins match ours
yet we say we're not related at all

they feel, right?

they inhale hurt
they screech during arsons
their roots deeper than ours won't allow them to run
but we will
to the next one
& the next one

and the next one, right?

THIS IS A THREAT
(NOT A WARNING)
TO THE FASCISTS

Hark! Know that you cannot stop me
from deciding to pull the comforter over my head & shield myself
from the morning sun

You cannot stop me
from shedding tears at random places at random times

You cannot stop me
from loving who I love, kissing who I kiss, wanting what I want

You cannot stop me
from hoping for something better for both me & you

You cannot stop me
from fighting for a future worth fighting for

You will not stop a movement stronger than your hate

Alexis Jaimes, proud son of Mexican immigrants, resides in Santa Ana, CA. He just published his first chapbook through Bottlecap Press, "*Corazón Coalesced.*" His works have also been previously featured in *Polemical Zine, Alegría Magazine, Loud Coffee Press, San Diego Poetry Annual, Moon Tide Press, ¡Pa'lante!* and *MUSE Literary Journal.*

RADICALS

We've been taken over by radicals.
No, not the Feminists,
who burned their bras,
and terminated their pregnancies,
and called for the end of male supremacy.
No, not the Black Power Movement,
who grew their hair out long and proud,
who held their fists up high,
who sought the end of racial capitalism.
No, not the Progressives,
who chained themselves to trees,
who punctured holes in pipelines,
who believe in the redistribution of wealth
as the only means of a healthy, prosperous future.
No, these radicals are white,
these radicals are male,
these radicals are rich.
These radicals are using religious fundamentalism
to speak to the fears of an unenlightened populace.
These radicals are doubling down
against the cries for equality for all,
against the Feminists,
against the Black Power Movement,
against the Progressives and their socialist agenda.
These radicals are not who we are
or want to be,
but they are in power
and in need of nobody's blessing
to do as they want,
to do as they will.
And only a gathering of past radicals
joining forces, linking arms,
surrounding their fortresses
and calling for an abolition,
a reckoning of all the wrongs committed
and those committed still,
a revolution of the hearts and minds
of a nation under siege...
will force their hand.
And we will see
whose future is worth dying for.

KURT NEWTON

LET'S START A WAR

Let's start a war,
let's mobilize our troops
and aim our guns
at the enemy:
poverty,
disease,
injustice.

Let's start a war,
let's kill discord,
let's bury our differences,
let's build a wall to keep out
mischaracterization,
misunderstanding,
mistrust.

Let's start a war,
let's shoot for the stars
let's ignite the imaginations
of our children
with missiles of hope,
let's explode the myth
that a future like this
can't be possible.

Let's start a war
to end all wars,
let's murder hate,
let's lynch racism,
let's tear the heart
out of terrorism,
let's drown the world
with a deluge
of mutual respect
and love.

Kurt Newton's poetry has appeared in More Alternative Truths, Alternative Truths: Endgame, Alternative Leadership, Shout: An Anthology of Resistance, and Fumptruck

WHEN THE DEVIL ENTERS THROUGH THE DOOR

When the devil comes through the door,
the windows open by themselves,
and everything turns upside down!

When the devil comes through the door,
the bed turns into a grave,
the bathroom becomes kitchen,
the house gets filthy!

When the devil comes through the door,
You can run and hide in hell,
Because the devil's moved out!

KUR DJALLI HYN NGA DERA

Kur djalli hyn nga dera
dritaret hapen vetë
qumështi bëhet kos
gjithçka përmbyset

Kur djalli hyn nga brenda
jastëku bëhet gur
banjoja bëhet kuzhinë
shtëpia nevojtore

Kur djalli hyn nga dera
më mirë t'i marrësh plaçkat
të ikësh nga aty
të shkosh në rrotë të samës

CLOWN TIME

In this nebula of paradoxes
Man has lost his shadow
Stupid at the crossroads of life
Faces with the dilemma in the head:
guess which way the shadow went!

Mediocre faces in broken mirrors
They reflect the characters of hypocrites
That snatch everything they see on the ground.

A coin spins in the space of fate
While the clowns are squinting and slobbering
They eagerly await which side she will fall on.

Risk plays with short-sighted people
Until they are busy with the game of chance
They persistently search for its meaning.

This formula was not found for thousands of years
It will still be the same
And man will remain the same as he was
Waiting foolishly at the crossroads of life
With the dilemma in his head: guess which way his shadow went!

FARUK BUZHALA

KOHË KLOUNËSH

Në këtë mjegullnajë paradoksesh
Njeriu ka humbur hijen e vet
I budallepsur në udhëkryqin e jetës
Përballet me dilemën në kokë:
athua në cilën anë hija i shkoi!

Fytyra mediokrësh në pasqyra të thyera
Reflektojnë karaktere hipokritësh
Që zhvasin çdo gjë që shohin mbi dhe.

Në hapësirën e fatit rrotullohet një monedhë
Ndërsa klounët syshkoqur e gojëjargur
Me padurim presin se në cilën anë ajo do të bie.

Risku luan me njerëzit shkurtpamës
Derisa të marrosur janë me lojën e fatit
Kërkojnë me këmbëngulje kuptimin e saj.

Me mijëra vite nuk u gjet kjo formulë
Edhe aq do të venë e prap e njëjta gjë
E njeriu do mbetet po ashtu siç ishte
Duke pritur i budallepsur në udhëkryqin e jetës
Me dilemën në kokë: athua në cilën anë hija i shkoi!

Faruk Buzhala is a contemporary poet and writer from Kosovo.
He is known for his distinctive style of poetry, often exploring
themes related to identity, memory, and the human experience.
Buzhala has published several poetry collections and has
gained recognition for his work both in Kosovo and
internationally. His poems are characterized by their depth,
emotion, and evocative language, resonating with readers
through their profound reflections on life and society. Buzhala's
contributions to literature have established him as a prominent
figure in the literary scene of Kosovo and the wider Albanian-
speaking world.

I Was So Naive

I was so naive when I got to Berkeley
        politically at least
in 1966:
        Vietnam un-war drafting left and right
        Freedom of Speech Movement going on two years
        the Delano Grape Strike six months old
And I knew nothing of this – these things
        the state of the world
        the center of the world – Berkeley.
        two years before MLK was shot
        or Bobby.
They had not touched Southwestern at Memphis
        even though JFK was gone.

I had just spent a year in Spain
        "25 AÑOS DE PAZ CON FRANCO,"
the joke being *Ese Omo*
        [laundry detergent brands]
there was nothing clean about *that man*

Pain had propelled me to California
        not politics.
Had I expected to know California speak
        just because I was fluent in Spanish?
It didn't translate
        but I'm quick with languages.

My friends from the South were enlisting:
        inspired by jobs, possible careers,
maybe even some patriotism;
        my brother was paying his dues to the Air Force
                                for his education at West Point

Not so many had died yet in 1966.
I soon found my new friends
        amazingly innovative
in their methods of avoiding the draft
        and learned the reasons why.

I went to one demonstration
        at the Oakland Induction Center
where a young cop
        probably my age
        no doubt as scared as I was
almost pushed me through a plate glass window
        on an order through his earphone

Isabell VanMerlin

to rush us *disorderly disruptive riffraff,*
    scare us off;
get us the heck off the street
    of their beat.
We weren't riffraff.
    We didn't want to lose our lives,
the opportunity to get an education,
    the possibility of normal life
as an adult
    fighting some greedy, fat-cats' war.

I knew at that moment
    demonstration was not the way
to achieve peace –
    not even a peaceful demonstration.

Fear is great –
    the great motivator
Were we even scarier
    because we weren't violent?

And the fear of my physical safety did nothing
    to assuage my rage at the injustice
of just about everything.

How do you see the good behind war,
    violence, mayhem
the oppression of laborers
    that has nothing to do with justice or the people-
of harmony-
    much less life and prosperity?

How can there be solidarity
    when nothing is solid
or constant
    but fear?

DEPOSE

Were any workers ever deposed
to give statements on
our side of the story
      of
          well, life –
I guess that would be the subject
of this class action suit
for us petitioners.

What if there were a court of Justice
      somewhere
[not likely any justice on this planet]
and there were cases brought forward
on justice in the work place?
Are not all places, workplaces –
      at least in this country?

Are not all people workers?
      [at least from my perspective]

And before you start thinking
those fat cats on the top of the heap
certainly don't work
the way you and I probably think of
      work:
like getting your hands dirty
lifting heavy bales
being a hod carrier
or a tea picker
lost from sight
in a tea plantation
or a grape or lettuce picker –

but the fat cats in their suits
sitting behind their chrome and glass
      desks
or is some kind of precious wood from
the depleted rain forests now the fad
that they put their feet up on
      after the Martini lunches?

Can you imagine the amount
      of fear
it takes to do the work
that assuages the greed, ambition, iron facade
to make a CEO, a General, a billionaire?

ISABELL VANMERLIN

Do they get any joy
or release
or relief
or satisfaction
from a good fuck?
It's hard work
          for some.

I think I'd rather pick grapes.

But to get back to the title –
how many people
would we have to depose
to start shedding
some light of justice
on workers?

What court would we go to?
          Who would be the judge?

Isabell VanMerlin started writing poetry in 2008 from attending Speak Up!, the open mic, in Lynn, Massachusetts, and couldn't just listen. She started her own open mic in 2013, in Newburyport. Isabell edited and compiled eight anthologies for Merrimac Mic. She continues to teach Creative Writing and edits and formats books for others – her passion. Ms. VanMerlin has published her own *Body Speak, dowsing the body*; *Love and Garlic, the deformative years*; *Turkish Odyssey*, and has been published in many anthologies, and periodicals.

WORKERS UNITE

There are no Guarantees
1917 Russian Revolution brought great hope
Inspired workers around the world

Fighting back against the greed, corruption and genocide
Fighting for basic needs food, clean water, housing
Health Care, social Justice, equal rights, freedom of sexuality

As if in a nightmare
Where one watches the same movie
Over and over again
Workers coming together
Seeing their strength in collectively organizing
Unions, collective bargaining
Asking to receive the fruits of their labor
The violence, the thugs brought in to intimidate and kill
Suppression of the workers on strike

The movie might seem on repeat
As the years go by the means of production changes
The system of unregulated capitalism is out of control
We keep hoping for a leader of the people
Believing in a system that is rigged

How have we lost our confidence in our own leadership
Why do we keep waiting for someone else
To lead us
Why aren't we leading ourselves collectivity

There has been a long history of
Unions, worker owners, collective cooperative ownership
Having control over means of productions
To produce goods and services needed by the workers

It is obvious we need to
Eliminate CEOs, management and investors exorbitant profits
Eliminate venture capitalist liquidating companies
Destroying and using up all available resources
For capital gains with no accountability
While putting workers and families in poverty and homeless

There has been a long history
Of fighting for the crumbs
Being blinded of our collective needs
Blaming others instead of seeing a rigged system
Based on confusion, hate and suppression

PAUL RICHMOND

The rich are not our heroes
Not to be looked up to
There have been victories
Yet the greed and power hungry
Sprout up when we stop being vigilant
Without demanding accountability
They run amuck with our future
They must we stopped

We need more than hope
We need to find our moral compass
Organize, dismantle the systems of oppression
In our daily lives and in who we are
For a better life for future generations
There is work to be done
There are no Guarantees

Paul Richmond was awarded Beat Poet Laureate
by National Beat Poetry Foundation for, MA
2017-2019, USA 2019-2020, & Lifetime 2022.
Performs nationally and internationally, solo
and with "Do It Now." He has eight books, more
info www.humanerrorpublishing.com

THE WORKING ASS

Every day I get up and have to work
I struggle with my health issues
pay taxes and strive to make ends meet

Far away the tech oligarchs are kissing the ass of the white purge
at the greasy smorgasbord

The buffet table is rotten and benefits the elites
They serve a capitalist slipslop at a high price

I remind you that:
their decisions are made by goddammit and can't be changed
goddammit

They offer a combustible combo of neoliberal inferno:

being born in America – to the right kind of parents
– entitles them to do whatever
they can threaten different populations
invade countries and change their borders
support genocides
burn down lands to transform them in an AI – powered infrastructure

Their birthright has to be protected from anyone
especially from us,
the working ass

SERENA PICCOLI

In Memoriam - January 20th, 2025

The new boombastic president presidente presidentissimo issimo
habemus papam war lord of the new and the old and the future
colonies lord of the alibi chief marketing warmongering fast food
propaganda officer best in the universe leader lider maximo maximum
magnum further fuhrer duce dux fiat lux habemus pontificem et
dominum et cetera father of our souls director of our lives ante
meridiam and post meridiam principal of the financial and arm
production agenda per capita and per capital owner of the planets the
plants the power plants the palms and the prunes alias founder of the
universe universal megatron megalithic mega lithium megaloman maga
supreme superlative supersonic leader of all the fleas and the leeches
and his arslickers is back in charge to save us all
Amen

and god piss America

Serena Piccoli, is an Italian poet and playwright. She
lives in Italy. Her latest book of poems is PRUNES
AND PRISMS, written with William Allegrezza,
published by Lavender Ink in September 2024.
www.lavenderink.org/site/shop/prunes-and-
prisms/?v=a906dcd34dae She writes poems about
social injustices and contemporary issues. She
writes both in English and Italian. Her website:
serenapiccoli.wixsite.com/serenapiccoli

America, I'm Not Going Anywhere

America

I'm not going anywhere
I will not leave you
I stand with you

America

I pledge allegiance to the fearless ones
to the ones without bullshit
the truth tellers
who stand with me now
the ones who speak out against tyranny
who resist liars thieves hungry ghost hate filled tyrants

America

I pledge allegiance to freedom equality and justice for all people
including immigrants the poor the downtrodden the homeless
I pledge allegiance to empathy compassion
to resurrection of the heart

America

I pledge allegiance to my black brown red white rainbow
friends of all colors of all ethnicities and nationalities
friends of all beliefs non-beliefs religions and spiritualities
to my female male gay lesbian bisexual transgender straight friends
to children the elderly
to those who are unable to take care of themselves

America

I pledge allegiance to trees to green grass
to brown earth to wildflowers of every color
to wilderness to turquoise skies
to rivers lakes and seas
to healing the earth

America

I pledge allegiance to dreams
I pledge allegiance to birth the journey and to death

America

I pledge allegiance to candor sincerity honesty to truth
I pledge allegiance to passion to compassion
to empathy and to helping those in need

America

I pledge allegiance to resurrection of the heart
I pledge allegiance to resurrection of the heart

America

I pledge allegiance to being a non-violent peaceful poet
standing fearlessly on the frontlines
fighting for freedom equality and justice
for all people

America

I'm not going anywhere
I will not leave you
I stand with you
I stand with love

Ron Whitehead is a poet, writer, editor, publisher, professor, scholar, activist, and U.S. National Lifetime Beat Poet Laureate. Ron grew up on a farm in Kentucky, is the author of over 30 books and more than 40 albums.

Photo by Jinn Bug.

DEPORTING THE MUSES

My muses are awaiting deportation
They sit silent and dejected
on the floor of a frigid holding cell in Fall River
wrapped in Mylar blankets
Now we speak to one another briefly at prescribed times
through a thick wall of glass

I cannot offer them succor or hope
We all know what is going to happen

They used to sing to me
They gifted me with words and ideas
But now I am barren

Now poetry feels like drone footage of
burned out forests in California
Ashen, grey and still

Like the check engine light in my car
The machine works
But there is a problem

Our collective mind has been hijacked
with plaques and tangles
corroding and sabotaging the rule of law
assassinating compassion

When Anna Akhmatova was
waiting outside of the prison
for news of her son who was arrested
She was asked if she could describe this

I can, she replied.

Anna, I cannot.

Linda Werbner is a Salem, Massachusetts-based
therapist and writer. Her work has appeared in online
literary publications including Quail Bell, Oddball
Magazine, Jerry Jazz Musician Journal and Global
Poemic. When she's not sitting with clients and
practicing tikkun olam (healing the world), she enjoys
performing at spoken word open mics, making quilts for
loved ones and playing her banjo.

A Silent Revolution

Have you ever heard of a hummingbird?
an incessant fluttering of those wings
working tirelessly for their sustenance
a drop of nectar and more –
something to quench the thirst of a red-throated
that can flicker wings to an unimaginable speed
of 80 flickers per second

sometimes, silence screams the loudest –
as the spring arrives breaking hard pointy
sharp ends of that stubborn ice
jutting, melting everything in this way
breaking open the ice slabs so the river
can dance again with complete abandon
sometimes nature teaches us resilience
and strength in her ways

sometimes the silence of a hummingbird
as it sucks the next drop of sustenance
through her long bill without so much of
making a whisper and hush
teaches us that not all the revolutions
are loud and boisterous
not all battles are won on the frontlines
not every struggle is a struggle of life and death

sometimes we die slowly getting caught
in our own juxtaposition of emotions
trying to fly high in a world mapped
and charted by hands that don't belong to us

sometimes power comes
from the relentless fluttering of wings
against the turbulent power of wind
proving its omnipresence

sometimes you strive through life
slurping and sucking drops of nectar
thought the tall stalks of Foxgloves
slowly and surely –
as they stand mighty tall under the bright blue skies.

Megha Sood is an award-winning Asian-American author, poet, editor, and literary activist from New Jersey. Literary Partner with "Life in Quarantine," at Stanford University. Her four poetry collections include (My Body Lives Like a Threat, FlowerSong Press, 2022), (My Body is Not an Apology, FinishingLine Press, 2021), and (Language of the Wound is Love, FlowerSong Press, 2025). She has received support from VONA, Pen Women, Dodge Foundation, Kundiman, and Martha's Vineyard Writing Institute.

THE VERNAL POOL

The flag is twisted
And the vernal pool is dry
This November.
Rusty ribbons, cage-like, dripping,
Feeding strange roots.
Where does all the life go
When the drought comes?
Dried blood, the marsh looks burnt.
Something may have died in me.
Stripes and the field of blue stars
Reaching for the ground.
Wild flames are engulfing the nation
While I drive the back road
And the vernal pool
Is the epitome of sadness.
A savage sky sighs
Like it doesn't know what to do.
The aftermath of casting spells
That didn't count when tallied.
Maidens wait to be born
Of burned intentions.
The rain is gone.
We're not connected.
This "union" is a dried vernal pool
Where we search in this
Cold mud.
There's something in this mud.
There's something that's gone.
It's been drowned in the dry,
Caked, cracked, cold
November vernal pool
And I want to resist
And stick my feet in it.
I want us to be healed.
Where is the rain?

Claire Conroy, Beat Poet Laureate of Maine 2024-2026, has self-published two books of poetry ("Listen" in 2018 and "Silent" in 2022) and a chapbook ("Rumors From Dead Lips" in 2024). Born in Portsmouth, NH, she is a proud board member of the Portsmouth Poet Laureate Program and is the host of their open mic, The HOOT. She has been published in over 20 anthologies and has been translated into Hindi by Devesh Path Sariya. Claire's passion, in addition to writing both beat style and format poetry is reading poetry. With a deep appreciation for jazz poetry, she loves the opportunity to perform poetically with musicians. Claire holds poetry workshops in Sanford, Maine where she lives.

HOME OF THE ENSLAVED

No flag can demarcate
my home or identity.
No country I see can
be land of the free
while one million plus
remain in custody.

* poem written after reading "Prisoners in the US are part of a hidden workforce linked to hundreds of popular food brands" in The Chronicle-Telegram (29 Jan 2024)

DON'T FREEZE

Ice doesn't easily melt,
especially in Northeast Ohio,
but we need to help keep folk
from slipping, being broken.

Who better to tell us how we can
best assist than the people already
engaged in the essential work
at HOLA Ohio, a 501c3 nonprofit
empowering Latino families, workers,
and immigrants in our area through
education and community support.

There are things they want
concerned folk to know:

Though hurting communities are terrorized
they need to carry on their lives, their children's
lives, and spreading panic is not helpful.

"Know your Rights" posts preach
to the choir, ignore the complexity
of handling each unique situation.
Don't tell immigrants what to do.
Do something yourself.

Correct disinformation, tear down
dehumanizing stereotypes. People often fail
to stand up for immigrants because they believe
lies about them. And it keeps getting worse.
Do stand up for them.

Call your reps, express your concern,
tell them you value immigrants,
do not fear them.

Volunteers are swamped. Help them focus
on important challenges by taking things off
their plates like grant writing, event planning,
fundraising. Commit time, skills and money.

Donations to HOLA help those being held by ICE
with legal representation, funds for the commissary.

They also help with HOLA's operating costs.
Visit HOLAohio dot org to learn more.

But the problem is not confined to here,
so look for people and organizations
doing similar work in your area. Help them.

The ice will not easily break but we can help
people not drown beneath it. And we must.

John Burroughs is a West Virginia-born, Buckeye-bred poet
and publisher based in Cleveland, Ohio. He founded Crisis
Chronicles Press, served as Ohio Beat Poet Laureate (2019-21)
and U.S. Beat Poet Laureate (2022-23) and is currently 2nd
Vice President for the Ohio Poetry Association. Find him at:
https://linktr.ee/johnburroughs.

AFFIRMATIONS FOR JURY NULLIFICATION

Welcome to this space of courage, peace, and clarity.

Take a moment and adjust any preconceived thoughts as we begin.
Align to the spirit of the times and the needs of the many.

Breathe in a willingness to draw a line in the sand.
Breathe out your fear of corporations.

Let your mind open to affirmations designed
to guide you toward resilience and trust:

I release the tension of denied treatments
and medical assistance and allow certainty to flow through me.

I trust my inner wisdom to guide me toward progress.

With each breath, I let go of worry and embrace the balance
between the law and my conscience.

I am free to think critically and make choices aligned with justice.

I am calm. I am centered.

I release fear and welcome in the courage to stand by my beliefs.

In stillness, I use my voice and find the strength
to declare the verdict: not guilty.

TABITHA DIAL

Home Economics

Some of y'all
never created a
protest sign and
that should've been taught:

taxes, meal prep, laundry, solidarity
covered in one semester where

you must use bold face,
one to twelve words.

The message succinct, clear –
as though you only had as much room
as there is allowed
on three bullets.

Tabitha Dial wants you to create your fate. And wishes
that were simple. She won the Penned Literary Contest
with her poem "Green Soup" in 2021 and published her
first book, "Creative Divination: Read Tea Leaves and
Develop your Personal Code" in 2018. She lives in New
Jersey and "Solidarity Forever" is one of her favorite tunes.

CONSTANTLY RISKING ABSURDITY # 247

after Lawrence Ferlinghetti
for Illiterate Light

You take the loop to Thomas.
"One Hundred and eighteen more days," you said.
This wasn't your first rodeo.
Two truths and a lie.
You knew how to wrangle and bridle a horse,
the road, this poem –
Though, why ever do, lie – innocence? Deception? Mercy?
I'm totally fed up with lies.
Unlike perennials returning.
Unlike night of jazz last Friday and walk home in flurries.
Unlike fingertip dipped handwritten messages in freshly fallen snow
to whoever might walk past and look.
So – I woke early, drove three hundred miles west
ancient golden glowing in topaz night
monument and glyph to sandstone sun
to home of ocean –
Ancient ecological bones –
Where do you get your blue?
And why the great divide?
Allegheny bound, I cross through the
Greater Eastern Continental Divide,
through mountain foothills
to protected wetlands.
At least I keep you honest.
The statue at the VMFA could have my name on it
or yours, or your name, mine, which reads:
Ancient Ethereal Egyptian Scribe and who has been ordained by Thoth.
Whoever gets bored of these questions? Not me!
You stand there talking to it for hours
and forget all together its reflection in human form
Standing, dancing just behind you, having already gone before you
to make sure it was safe.

And, for you, it was –
even on snow kissed roads
You drove through the night three hours.
There stood some magic

in the mountains, the winter, its trees, the snow, the ice.
Wind even carried its beautiful breath
foregoing its bitter temperament
to say things plainly –
What will become of the eye
in the storm?
Maybe you?
Only God knows who holds the golden feather
and who drinks from the river,
An ancient Ibis or smoldering Sun god
carrying on

Ashby Logan Hill is a poet, writer, artist, and educator from Harrisonburg, VA currently living in Richmond. He has been blessed to study extensively with poets including James Tate, Dara Barrois-Dixon, Lynn Xu, Peter Gizzi, Camille Rankine, Lilah Hegnauer, and Laurie Kutchins and with writers including Hilary Holladay, Sabina Murray, Edie Meidav, Jeff Parker, Shastri Akella, and Noy Holland, among others. He holds an MFA in Poetry from UMASS Amherst (2017) where he was a reader for Jubilat. His work can be found in voicemail poems, WHURK Cultural Review, River City Poets Anthology, and the 2024 Virginia Poetry Society Anthology among other places.

A Question of Time

time is a man made measurement
of accomplishments to-do lists
wrinkles newborn cries holidays
we measure sun the moon our cycles
markers that fall precisely in lives

cake in the oven wedding date ahead
days until vacation hours and breaths

is it real or just imagined
methodical stacking of blocks
arranged order and disorder
how do we measure existence
does it happen length or content

is a butterfly whose life is shorter
any less pretty because of this

elephant more dear whose gestation
is longer than the human who rides it

a coin more precious than gold
our worth folded between sunsets
dropped in freshly opened eyes
left as a record when we breathe our last
overrated overlooked overmeasured

by natural rhythms of life
by those instincts we fight against

imagine if you will a world
with no markers where we are happy
with floating for the sake of it
where we are not weighted by the
ticks of a clock days of a calendar
Rita Spalding
The What Ifs

what ifs can push you to insanity
but they serve their purpose

sorting reasoning dividing conquering
what if winter storms never end

what if I get stuck in my mind
where all my fears dwell in puddles

what if we all go to hell in a basket
well at least we go together

in the world of heavy what ifs
we turn reality when we overthink

so what if we imagine the brilliant stars
shine so brightly that we can't see

darkness waiting to swallow us
what if there was always an ocean

waiting desperately for our splashes
what if we could swing our spindly legs

from the curve of a white crescent moon
and dance in the black sky that holds it

what if to be loved is out of reach
but we feel love touching us anyway

Rita S. Spalding has been published in 18 Calliope anthologies, National Library of Poetry, AX-POW Magazine, The Heartland Review, Kentucky Monthly Magazine, Keeping the Flame Alive, Fallen, Rebirth, The Rye Whiskey Review, and Walden's Poetry and Reviews. Her first book Abstract Ribbons was published in 1992. She has two books being published in 2025. Titles are What is Beauty and The Eighth. She has received awards for poetry from Jefferson Community and Technical College, Elizabethtown Community College, Kentucky State Poetry Society, Kentucky Monthly Magazine, National Library of Poetry, and was recently nominated for the Pushcart Prize in poetry. She has been writing for sixty four years, breathes and bleeds poetry, and gives readings regionally and nationally.

CRACK ANOTHER EGG

Come on now crack another egg
Let the golden yolk run
Crack another egg
And then another one

O for the poor coffee picker
You on twenty cups a day
O for the poor coffee picker
Please consider the working wage
Down in his little tin hovel
With not enough to eat
Down in the south American sun
By the mansion in the heat

He'd like to crack another egg
Let the golden yolk run
He'd like to Crack another egg
And then another one

He'd crack one for his momma
Crack one for his son
They'd sit round a great big table
And eat till they are strong

He should grow potatoes
Yes and he should grow rice
But coffee in America
– it brings a higher price
So he has to work so hungry
Picking coffee in the sin
When he see his bosses shiny white head
It makes him wonder how long – how long –

Before he Cracks another egg
Let the golden yolk run
Crack another egg
And then another one

He'd crack one for his son Eduardo
Crack one for the homophobes
Crack one for Fidel Castro
Crack for Mr. Jones
O crack for the Americans
And let us not forget
We all get our equal share
Of the omelet
You heard me Of the omelet

ROBERT PRIEST

HOW MUCH PATIENCE

how much patience does it take
to wait forever
and still get nothing
how much virtue in that
how many forms before you get the final
form letter of denial
a blank wall
uncrossable

how much patience does it take
when you are hungry
when you are angry inside
when you are going crazy
how much does it take
to finally get
the same old answer
as before

somewhere someone has got you by your children
got you by your organs
got you by the blood you need
or just plain food to eat
and you know clearly what must be done

how much patience does it take
to lie there bleeding
and watch it
not get done

Robert Priest is the author of fourteen books of poetry,
3 plays, 4 novels, lots of musical CDS, and one hit
song. His words have been debated in the legislature,
posted in the Transit system, quoted in the Farmer's
Almanac, and sung on Sesame street. His book:
Reading the Bible Backwards peaked at number two on
the Canadian poetry charts. His latest recording Love
is Hard is available on Spotify, YouTube and iTunes.
His most recent book: If I Didn't Love the River (2022).

Palm Sunday

the hood is draped in palms
all the believers
got a lot of praying to do
seems like the ancestors ain't pleased
mother earth is being disrespected
she's sending earthquakes, floods, droughts and tornadoes
y'all ain't listening though
seems like not enough was given up for lent
guns are out of control
karma for the west being stolen at gunpoint
the whole thing is gangsta
that's why Teflon Don has been indicted
there's a new sheriff in town
I ain' try'n to scare ya
but it's beginning to look like revelations up'n here
so whoever ya believe in
maybe it's time to say a prayer
it seems like shit is coming to an end

FUTURE

some think the future
doesn't look too good
but all time is now
and life is a cycle past/present/future
everything has it's seasons
but only man believes in time
so we pray that tomorrow
brings peace on earth
but was earth ever peaceful
perhaps this chaos is eternal
if you believe in time
it's only a man made illusion anyway
so there's no pay-by-the hour
what did we do before cash
what did beggars beg for
food insecurity wasn't invented
were only the dispossessed hungry
somewhere war is constant
conflict makes the world go round
I'm lookin for the Black Star Liner
to take me to a different universe
shape shift to a bird
and fly away`````````````````````

Ngoma Hill is a performance poet, multi-instrumentalist, singer/songwriter, Artivist and paradigm shifter, who for over 50 years has used culture as a tool to raise socio-political and spiritual consciousness through work that encourages critical thought. A former member of Amiri Baraka's "The Spirit House Movers and Players" and the contemporary freedom song duo "Serious Bizness," Ngoma weaves poetry and song that raises contradictions and searches for a solution to a just and peaceful world.

The Last Entry in the Journal of a Forgotten Man, December 24, 2125

Tomorrow we surrender our daughter to the overlord in exchange for this year of grace. An exemption after ten years of debt. Our bailiff says, "Jubilee Year," to mock my wife and me. "The biblical way" he snickers at my wife's despair. The overlords pick and choose their holiness. Their beatitudes and blessings. For weeks, my wife wept into the bitter soups we dine on at twilight. I offered my superiors a kidney and both eyes. To no avail. This morning our daughter butchered her copper hair. Now her skull looks manged, like the coats of the wild dogs that scavenge in the Valley of Refuse. At daybreak, the bailiffs will assemble before our door with a limousine and an escort of prosperity marines. They'll dress our daughter in black-and-gold regalia for the next competition. A beautiful face to celebrate the giants that were bred for the master's bally sports. With their hoops and clubs and time clocks. Until her limber fails. Until her somersaults and cartwheels collapse. She'll mare a decade for the gene designers who breed the next hall of famers and soldiers who obey the overlord's whims. After her last fallow, she'll disappear. Erased, even from the census. Our bailiff granted me this boon after I agreed to triple my production of whatever products they require. Ammunition, hero dolls of past oligarchs, plastic food. Or else our sons will be forfeited to the forever wars – martyrs who will lead assaults into cities in rebellion. And brave the moats of mine fields and waste the small arms fire of the resistance. Tomorrow I begin my labors, 16-hour days in the furnaces. Forbidden to watch the prosperity marines wrest our first child away.

Michael Brockley is a retired school psychologist who lives in Muncie, Indiana. His prose poems have appeared in Red Eft Review, The Prose Poem, and Unlikely Stories Mark V. Brockley's prose poems are also forthcoming in Ley Lines Literary Review and Keeping the Flame Alive.

L'Océan

Tous les ruisseaux du monde
finissent par rejoindre la mer...
Peut-être,
dans l'avenir,
existera-t-il un océan commun
où pareillement
tous les ruisseaux humains
pourront se réunir.

The Ocean

All the streams in the world
end by reuniting with the sea...
Perhaps,
in the future,
there will exist an ocean for all
where in the same way
all the human streams
will be able
to reunite with each other

* Translated from French by Barbara Paschke

Francis Combes founded the press "Le Temps des Cerises," from the title of a well-known song of the Commune de Paris. He left it in 2021. He was also the organizer of a campaign of poetry posters in the Paris'Metro, for fifteen years. He launched a call for a Worldwide chain of poems for Peace. As a poet, he has published more than 30 books, including Cause commune, le Cahier bleu de Chine, La France aux quatre vents, Lettres d'amour porte restante, La face cachée de la Lune. His work has been translated into English, Spanish, Arabic, German, Italian, Macedonian, Albanian, and Chinese. He has translated into French books by Heinrich Heine, Vladimir Mayakovsky, Attila Jozsef, and Jack Hirschman.

Barbara Paschke translates from Spanish and French. Her publications include Riverbed of Memory (Daisy Zamora); Volcán; Clandestine Poems (Roque Dalton); Clamor of Innocence; Tomorrow Triumphant (Otto Rene Castillo); New World, New Words; To the Left of the Heart; literary travel companions to Costa Rica, Cuba, and Spain, and six anthologies from the Revolutionary Poets Brigade. She has served as board member and conference organizer for the American Literary Translators Association (ALTA) and is on the board of the Center for the Art of Translation.

WELCOME TO THE THIRD WORLD!

Oh, my dear America, where shall we start?
Perhaps with your name, who named you that way?
Were they expecting to unite all of the continent, Bolivar style?
All the countries in the American Continent united,
wouldn't that be nice?
Except, not under Uncle Sam's boot.
Not under his undermining moods...
    Touch and destroy.
    Desire and destroy.
    If it can't be mine, destroy?!
    Because the only way to do things, is mine, of course!

Such is your thought, your "Manifest Destiny."
To impose on others and show them how
to do, to be, to punish, to exist.
    Entertain and destroy.

Outside, I mean, outside your borders,
you are seen as mean and hypocritical
A nation built by slaving fathers and hushed mothers.
A nation built by fleeing puritans and impoverished derelicts.

But also by daring daring and formidable souls,
full of lust and greed for riches, for knowledge, discovery,
of course, fame, and above all, power.
The power to become like God:
to name, build create, transform,
but above all,
destroy.

Oh, America, the beautiful, America the brave
You do more than ignore brothers and sisters of darker color skin
or Earthlier thoughts and practices.
You intent to suppress by ghettoing them
and any seemingly opposing "other",
separating everyone by class and race.
And above all, by money.
"Whitening" force imposed on us
for Queen, King or Pope, or any other "royal" or "divine" reason.

Not all survive nor can resist you, America.
Seemingly brilliant colonizer as you were, once.
Not everyone believes the stories you produce
in order to distract us and everyone else in the world.

Hypnotized by the likes of Hamelin Obama,
You have yielded your mind
Fed, drunk, stoned, comfy and entertained.
And yes, it is disheartening to witness

PILAR RODRÍGUEZ ARANDA

the deafness and blindness of your government,
its constant denial, its lack of humility.

Citizens, you've been fooled by your leaders.
Purposefully misled, to feel fear
And believe the simplified world of lies
embedded since childhood
by education and surrounding voices
For God and Profit, what's not to like?

I'm not sure if you have really seen
What's going on within you
Your homeless families
Your obese electorate
Censoring and bigot news media and teachers.
It's all falling apart
Not sure if there's time to fix

But there's one thing I would advise
Only one, for now
Do not try to heal the wound
using the same old remedies
sugarcoated with lies and debris
of past dreams gone sour

> *Desire and destroy*
> *If it can't be mine*
> *– like a real spoiled baby –*
> *I'll destroy it*
> *Because the only way to do things*
> *is mine, of course!*

How can you America, be the only one allowed
to put holes, print shadows, impose hunger
pile mass shootings, poison your citizens 'water?
Turn them into deformed, exploited, exploded bodies

Oh America it moves me, your naïveté
Your eyes not comprehending when or why
The "most powerful" country in the world got lost
Or rather, forgot to look within and
Acknowledge the suppuration of its wounds

Your founding creeds denied, as they were only words
Your initial essence corrupted, as it was only a façade

And now, you are mostly weak, thrashed, interrupted
A regular "Third World" dive

So, welcome!

The time has come to transform
To "die" is to evolve, *America...*

News vs. Stories

A child dies holding on to his dog
surrounded by an infinite hell
Roaring flames melting metal and lungs
– exceeding agony
Unfair and incomprehensible
stupidity

News looking for poetry
Images in search of a cause
Looking not for rhyme but to provoke
Indignation? Rage?
Subordination exchange...

A shocking tragedy
converted into a ribbon
black, yellow, untied

We're addicted to the bittersweet formula
of intriguing sex and spattering blood
of extreme danger and young desire
with no aftereffects

Even after a pancaked Miami Condo
or any other unannounced tragedy
obviating ever-lasting corruption

After thousands bombed, unrooted
Starved
Frail and undecided
What can anyone do?
Many have lost the way
back to humanness

If we were to absorb all the "news"
React to each one
Do something about it all
most likely we would collapse
under such–fastidious–weight

I'd rather help thread a multicolor braid
In a strange gathering of hope
after so much loss
Life itself, a daily aftershock
The constant return of the wave

If we could allow ourselves to feel
the rain falling hard, drench ourselves
of its liquid generosity
Nourish our empathy

Kindness survives misery
and stories remain
So, retell the old stories, forget a bit
about "the news"

Sing, recite or dramatize
with a reasoned end in mind
and clarity in your message
Help it become a magnificent jewel!

Craft your voice and free the tale

Once, I was privileged to one such story
In some video…

A sick, delirious man
takes off one of his layers,
an old stinking shirt
Patiently, he puts it on another man
who's naked on the chest
Then, from his bag
he brings out a beanie
to cover the bold head
of his less fortunate
new friend for life.

Pilar Rodríguez Aranda (Mexico, 1961) A writer and multidisciplinary artist born in Mexico. She lived 13 years in the USA and has been a Tijuana borderlands resident since 2016. Honored as International Beat Poet Laureate in 2021, Rodríguez Aranda has published in more than a hundred magazines and anthologies, and her poetry has been translated into various languages. She has been part of various poetry festivals in Mexico, United States, Brazil, Ecuador, Italy, Cuba and Egypt. Her books can be purchased through Amazon. She started doing video art in college, received grants and won several prices in the nineties. Her work has been shown in festivals and museums in the European and American continents.

American John

Unrighteous laws, persecution, the denial of freedom
free to simply be ourselves. All of us

how can we judge? How can we see the splinter
in someone else's eye from the walls

we've built around? Oh, did you think
I was gonna get all holy on you?

Nah, if you're feeling damned
then that's just you, damning yourself.

We have enough obstacles in this life
to not go tripping each other up.

But people be trippin', all "Holier than thou!"
When you know, when I know, when we all know

none of us, I said none of us, are any better
than the next. Unrighteous laws, persecution

our lack of freedom. Yes, ours!
Because they won't stop, these hypocrites

that make the most shameful deals in the dark.
They crave power, they get off on control.

And right now, my friends, they're having an orgy
at our expense. If we let them rule one of us

then we let them rule us all. This denial of freedom
this persecution, these unjust laws.

A red, white and blue prostitute named "America"
and all of us it's John.

No matter how they try to spin it
we just keep getting fucked!

STRUNG OUT

I gotta get my fix. Earn some money so I can pay my rent.
I gotta find a job that's legit. I GOT BILLS TO PAY!

No more hustling in the streets, no more slinging dope.
No more good kush stink, trading time for smoke.

I GOT BILLS TO PAY! I gotta drug test to take
you know what I mean. I need that 401k, I gotta take care of me.

I gotta try to be the American dream. I GOT BILLS TO PAY!
I gotta get my fix, before the bottom drops out of all of this.

Before this paper money ain't worth a shit.
You know it scratches my ass when I wipe with it.

I GOT BILLS TO PAY! That's why I sacrifice my dreams
for this all-mighty dollar. Can you hear me holler?

I GOT BILLS TO PAY! Because in America none of us are free. We're all
slaves to the grind, slaves to the greed.

I GOT BILLS TO PAY! I gotta find a job real quick, with insurance
vacation, all that good shit. I GOT BILLS TO PAY!

The landlord keeps banging on my door, he wants his rent.
But all my money is already spent. God almighty

I GOT BILLS TO PAY! I gotta find a job that's legit
so, I can get my fix. Because I'm jonesing for those

dirty dollar banknotes. They ain't real money, they're a fucking joke.
WE ALL GOT BILLS TO PAY!

Living day by day, strung out in the U.S. of A.

Michael E. Duckwall was born and raised in the Ohio Valley. A featured poet at the 10th "Final" Gonzofest in 2023, he took off and hit the ground running as part of the production team for a 57hr non-stop "Insomniacathon" music and poetry event in Louisville KY 2024. Michael's poetry, artwork and photography have been in a handful of magazines and anthologies, along with numerous online features. He has a couple of chapbooks "Ramblings of a Recovering Poet" & "7.2 SkullQuake" in publication and one limited edition co-authored chapbook you may have missed out on. Michael's also the host of a monthly Open Mic in Scottsburg IN.

Neoliberal Spell

I curse you hunger
mother of all violence
Daughter of all corruption
                and all those sick
From the offices of corporations
Governments
and their banks
Their banks that swallow up
little by little
Your house,
my bag
and all our lives
I curse you violence
Daughter of all those who want us docile
and quiet
And fill us with hunger and discourage
to continue unpunished
Their reign.
I curse you western
white history
For normalizing your crimes
and wars
And leave the second
eating our wine
drinking of our bread
I curse you
comfortable silence
you cover us
with the same blanket
The same one
that suffocates all of us
While others own our oxygen
and drink little by little
all we call our small
allowed
"Freedom".

Vanessa Torres (Bogota, Colombia 1978): Colombian poet and cultural anthropologist, graduated from the Universidad Nacional de Colombia, Master in Spanish studies and linguistics from the Universidad Pontificia de Salamanca, currently resides in San Francisco, California, USA. Creator, feminist and cultural activist, she has worked on the projection of Hispanic American culture as well as the visualization of the arts and literature made by women creators, inside and outside the United States through radio, journalism and literature. Her poetry and literary journalism projects have been published in literary magazines in Spain and the United States.

THE ANTI-POETS

we are the anti-poets
we don't need no stinking badges
our poems are served up like mashed potatoes
with hamburg gravy
wash 'em down with cheap beer
onions are like apples to us
we don't even peel them
just bite into them out of hand
we don't like your foo foo prancing
we want to punch your head
and tell you to wake the fuck up
and if we hear one more beach poem
about seashells from your MFA program
we will march on your homes and steal your women
god damn it grow some fucking balls
scream at the fucking sky
get a grip
stop kissing everybody's ass
with your pussy foot nonsense
don't you have anything to say?
that isn't some kind of pandering tripe
la de da dee fucking da
and cut the shit with this serious concern
about the homeless   or the blacks
or the gays   or the native americans
or the migrants   or the working class
or the jews   or the palestinians
or the veterans   or the war
or the victims of sexual abuse
or whatever else you claim to feel sorry for
when we all know you couldn't care less
up there in ivory freakin' tower sucking the corporate teat
staring down at the unwashed uneducated masses
calling us stupid
we are the anti-poets
coming up out of the ground like stinkweed
and we are calling you out
on your bullshit

Tommy Twilite is a Massachusetts troubadour who combines music, poetry, exploration and adventure into his performances. He is the co-founder and director of the Florence Poets Society and the host of the Twilite Poetry Pub on WXOJ Valley Free Radio. His latest chapbook, "Kills No Bird" is a follow up to his 2021 collection, "Fifty Words for Rain". Tommy is the editor of the Silkworm annual review, and is a Lifetime Beat Poet Laureate. He believes poetry and song can renew the Earth.

Programmed

When you were born they gave you a number
A number that determines your blood type
Determines which school you're going to attend
Which troop you're going to belong to
Which job you're going to take
With whom you're going to get married
Whom you're going to serve
In front of whom you`re going to dance
In front of whom you`re going to whine
You`ve been programmed!

Programirani

Kad si se rodio dobio si broj
Koji određuje tvoju krvnu grupu
Koji određuje u koju ćeš školu
Koji određuje u koju ćeš trupu
Koji određuje na koji ćeš posao
Koji određuje s kim ćeš da se ženiš
Koji određuje koga ćeš da služiš
Pred kim ćeš da igraš
Pred kim ćeš da šeniš
Ti si zauvek programiran!

Vasa Radovanović was born 196 in Belgrade (Serbia). He published five books of poetry. His poems are translated into and published in the following languages: French, English, Japanese, Turkish, German and Russian. He is the member of Society of Serbian writers.

COMMUNISM WILL WIN

My first Christmas sober
And I am having some difficulty
Family around the table
And I am somewhere else
I don't mean to be distant
It's just my mind is always racing
And it takes a lot to slow it down
Somone's grandfather
Is off in the corner
And he is drinking
And he is over one hundred
And he is alone
And I think to strike a conversation
He tells me
He remembers me
He is quite lucid
Tells me of his history
The cities
He had known
Some he had loved
Tells me of his love for Mexico
Tells me of his for the people
Tells me that he is a liberal
Then with a smirk
And a forming tear
If you pushed him
He was a communist
I tell him
So am I
He tells me
Not to tell anyone
I tell him
It's too late for that
The tears are now fully formed
My own run down cheek
He turns and looks to the children
Tells me we will win
It is only a matter of time

Matt Sedillo has been described as the "best political poet in America" by investigative journalist and documentarian Greg Palast as well as "the poet laureate of the struggle" by Professor and Historian Paul Ortiz. Sedillo's work has drawn comparisons in print to Bertolt Brecht, Roque Dalton, Amiri Baraka, Allen Ginsberg, Carl Sandburg and various other legends of the past.

Lest - Together Rise by the Fiery Winds Call!

Though mine heart was broken not;
In half-and-half was weighed –
Upon these scales – that truth had sought,
Yet – stood – in silence – in all ways!

Though mine heart was broken not;
It was found divided as so –
Holding time – times – caught,
Not knowing anymore tomorrows –

Though mine heart was broken not;
It was found divided by fire and sea,
That is to say – with speech it taught –
The fowls words – its prophecy!

Though mine heart was broken not;
It was found between life and death –
With cardinals six in number that wrought
The word of life – what is – is not – in its breath!

Though mine heart was broken not!
Side by side – did stand –
Counting – times – time had bought,
As stars within mine hand!

Though – mine heart was broken not!
Side by side – did vowels in half fall,
That speech be made moveable naught –
Lest – together – rise by the fiery winds call!

Katrenia Grace Busch is a freelance journalist whose work has appeared in NPR, CBS, as well as local newspapers. Her award-winning poem titled, "*Mystery and Wind*" took 2nd place in the 2022 League for Innovative Creative Writing contest. She continues to serve as a poetry editor for The Bookends Review and is on the editorial board for the American Psychological Association's Psychology of Consciousness: Theory, Research and Practice. She is a federal grant reviewer for the U.S. Department of Justice. Her work can be found in *Red Penguin Books, Bloom Magazine, The Trouvaille Review, October Hill, Literature Today* amongst others.

WHEN MIDNIGHT COMES

when midnight comes i will lift a cup in a crowded room because it is new year's and that means new hope and the delicious amnesia of smoke and mirrors of wine and witty forgetfulness;

i will lift a cup to rounded shoulders and worn out hair and empty my eyes and plant my feet firmly on god's good and familiar and disappointed earth, and for a couple of hours not feel the ground shake or bear witness to the graves desecrated or the vineyards robbed;

i will allow my attention to drift from face to face in search of a friend or lover i never once let down or who never let me down and anyhow let bygones be bygones and put aside all that has been half-forgotten;

i will lift a cup and find some rhythm or musical phrase or detail in the dead-ass room, some sign of life to sway my dying soul, some promise in the vaudeville and malingering, put aside the politics and restlessness and fresh inhumanities, rediscover the one urge the world is not yet hip to and never will be until it is probably too late, old as the world and not yet exhausted or wasted;

i will go through rooms of strangers and laugh and sweat and curse, i will share the same slogans and the same jokes, i will swap the same tears and insincere kisses, i will shrug off the usual errors and cheap shots and celebrate the extraordinary and the delusional;

i will sing a last new song, put aside the inventory of miscalculation and heartbreak; i will stop for one hour the counting of human cost and casualties; i will go through rooms and rooms i no longer wish to travel in and never much inhabited anyhow except in pursuit of unfulfilled desire, and welcome in the new year and set off fireworks and dance;

and attend to my underground dreams, and lift another cup to my lips; and celebrate the bitter fruits of the working man's love and labor, and be glad

AT THE SLAUGHTERHOUSE
OF THE INNOCENT

They displayed his body in the copper mines, they displayed his body in the laundry houses; they displayed his body in the slaughter pen and prison dining hall; to the children of the mad, the children of the innocent, the orphans and the disenchanted and the damned; they hung his face on shit-stuccoed walls and on the front pages of big city magazines; they whispered into the ear of the leper in his leper's bed, and the widow at the grave; we have killed him! we have killed him!

they marched in victory parades, they hung banners in the branches of the tipuana tipu tree; they displayed his body naked as a hillside, naked as a light bulb, bullet-ridden and listless as a side of beef on a butcher's rack; but they could not kill him; because he was confident to the last, and wide as a continent, even in death, with his poetry and his love and his patient, working man's hands; and the people whispered, he is alive, he is still alive!

because the people are stubborn as mud and straw, stubborn as a pool of blood on the side of a government highway; because the people tell truths no one else will tell, if only to teach each other, beneath deafening skies; because warplanes can streak victorious across the face of heaven all day long if they want to but they cannot cast shadows over pure men's hearts; because he was their victory and they knew it, they snatched him from the mouth of defeat;

because he was live as soil to them, their soil, no one else's; live as seed, live as hope; live as the fruit of the aichuchura tree.

George Wallace (b.1949 NY, USA), Writer in residence, Walt Whitman Birthplace. Author of 42 chapbooks and 5 spoken word albums in US, UK, Italy, Greece, Macedonia, Portugal, Saudi Arabia, India, Spain. Major international poetry festival prizes and appearances, inc. Orpheus Prize (BG); Alexander Prize, Aristotle Medal (GR); Silk Road Prize, Poet of the Year (CN); Naim Frasheri Laureateship (MK); Corona d'Oro (AL); Naji Naaman Literary Prize (LB), Medellin (CO, Ledbury (GB), Lyric Recovery/Carnegie Hall (US). National Beat/Next Generation Beat Poet (US); Honorary Doctorate, CiESART/Royal Academy 2024 (SP).

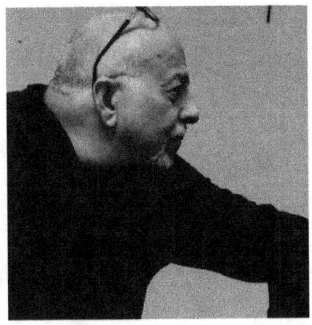

罗马的骡马

有的人一出生就在罗马
有的人一出生就是骡马
你看着峨眉山的骡马
背上驮着千斤的重物
脚下踏着潮湿的石阶
前方是峨眉山的大佛
山顶上的人等着供养
骡马不知道大佛
不知道被谁驱赶
山下的骡马食不果腹
山上的人们挥金如土
骡马的皮肤冒着汗
骡马的蹄子渗着血
实在爬不上去也只能硬抗
家里还有一家老小要养着
直到某天爬不动了
在石阶上轰然倒下
静悄悄地死去
让人宰杀成肉
就像从未出现过
峨眉山的骡马，人世间的骡马
世界的普罗大众看着不语
峨眉山的骡马，人世间的骡马
世界的普罗大众可曾明白？

THE MULES OF ROME

Some people are born as gentlemen in Rome
Some people are born as mules in China
You look at the mules in Mount Emei
Carrying a thousand pounds of heavy weight on its back
Stepping on damp stone steps underfoot
Ahead is the Giant Buddha of Mount Emei
The people on the mountaintop are waiting to be fed
Mules don't know the Buddha
Mules don't know who drove itself away
The mules at the foot of the mountain are starving
The people on the mountain spend money like dirt
The skin of mules is sweating
The hooves of mules are oozing blood
If he can't climb up, he can only resist hard
There is still an old and young family to take care of at home
Until one day he couldn't crawl anymore
Falling down on the stone steps with a loud crash
Quietly die, quietly die
People would slaughter it into meat
Just like never exist in the world
The mules of Mount Emei, the mules of the human world
The people of the world looks speechless
The mules of Mount Emei, the mules of the human world
Has people of the world ever understood?

Cao Shui (born in Jun 5, 1982), is a Chinese poet, novelist, screenwriter and translator. He is a representative figure of Chinese Contemporary Literature. He leads the Great Poetry Movement. His most notable works includes Epic of Eurasia, the already mentioned trilogy and King Peacock (TV series). So far 42 books of Cao Shui have been published, including 10 poem collections, 5 essay collections, 10 novels, 4 translations, 18 fairy tales and one hundred episodes TV series and films. He has won more than 50 literary awards worldwide. His works have been translated into 26 languages. He is also chief editor of Great Poetry, deputy editor in chief of World Poetry, secretary general of Boao International Poetry Festival  and chairman of the Beijing Poetry Film International Poetry Festival. Currently he lives in Beijing, and works as a professional writer and screenwriter.

THE COLD EYE OF THE BORDER MAN

It is dusk and the birds
have found their way home,
needless of a clock, map or sextant,
safe in their nests with a little brood

Things left behind
against circumstances are visualized
Voices resound in the convolutions of the brain
Curling to reach the ones who left
but they remind themselves of the chasm.

Now you are here
on the closest border
The border man will fix you
with the cold eye of a snake
and answer not a word
He will count you and give you a number
amongst the lucky ones
who left everything behind:
your scarves, robes, dresses and makeup
your silver, gold and bills
your freshly cut flowers,
your porcelain pots and pets,
your peevish and discredited gods.

What good is your clinging to unforgotten beauty?
What about the kinsmen and the lost friends?
Your rigorous bonds of blood
With their cold stares and blank faces?
They left your realm with its mundane prerequisites
They are now forming rings and joining hands
in games neither you nor your enemies know.

You said goodbyes and parted ways
in your different modern-day Sinais
You left everything behind
except your ancestral nightmares
born of Manichean doctrines
The border man will fix you with a cold eye,
count you and give you a number
You are just now the only lucky one.

EL HABIB LOUAI

FOR THOSE WHO PERISHED ON WAVES TO IMAGINED EL DORADOS

In my mind
I have a cold lake
Bigger than the one in the Atlas Mountains
The wind never stops blowing there
It is ruffled by the blood of those who perished
On the waves to imagined European El Dorados

I come to it stranger than before,
Not as a returning tourist from a bright city,
But as an eco-saint who tries to fathom
The hazy premises that show on my face

I come to it as an old native son, familiar with
the same marble patience that awaits change
I stand on my usual corner with my back to the world
I speak seldom to the watching pigeons
That I feed with what remains in my pockets
I roam thinking of the mothers who fight for breath
In the tumultuous pools of the seas,
The infants with tender skin, their elders' blind gaze
The ones who broker them to their slavers

I would like to believe in the Human Rights,
Divine justice and unexclusive mercy
As if savagery weren't the tongues
We have spoken since the beginning
When we started to think in terms of "nations"
For which humans sacrificed their young
Feasting in victory on their foes
Sticking figures on Capitol Hills
The same ones who claim right to Lifers,
Love for the mother sickly earth,
Read the Declaration of Independence
And mutter prayers to "the Son of God"

I walked away from the lake as I would
from myself and its despairs
How absurd, how vicious this world is!
There is nothing to do, but groan pathetically:
"To hell with your human needs and civilizing missions."

El Habib Louai is a Moroccan poet, translator, musician and assistant professor of English Literature at Ibn Zohr University, Agadir, Morocco. His research focuses on the cultural encounters, colonial discourse and postcolonial theory and he worked the Beats' archives at the University of North Carolina at Chapel Hill as a Fulbright grantee. He took creative writing courses at Jack Kerouac School of Disembodied Poetics at Naropa University, Boulder, Colorado where he performed with Anne Waldman and Thurston Moore.

#THEHOODISNOTFORSALE

Set the scene. Two characters, prospective lovers,
walk hand in hand through a park.
It's a pivotal scene in Hopscotch's opera,
a moment of calm between
the wild arcs of back story and foreshadowing.
The location was intentional too. Containing a lake,
it's a refreshing sight of green scenery amidst
the grey reality of the hood. Multi-generational homes,
front yards full of forgotten items placed to the side for space,
exist beside empty houses. New for sale signs in front of
rapidly aging fixer-uppers. Quaint mom-and-pop shops sit humbly
beside minimalist coffee shops. The architectural complexity
signifies change, a promising increase in property value.
Cars line the streets, parked up on the sidewalk.
Loud music thrums
from passing vehicles. The park is an escape for the lovers,
away from the bustle of life. Allowing
this moment of romance, their first kiss.
Trumpets blare, a dissonant melody to the scene
unfolding. The focus turns away from the lovers
and to a group entering the park. Not a part of the
performance, the new arrivals startle the performers and audience.
High schoolers blow into brass instruments creating
a muddled semblance of rehearsed music. Other residents
yell chants of rebellion. All in defense of a hood
too often used in an attempt to sell self-actualization to outsiders.
A fetishized fiction occupying the space of the people,
but no longer. The scattering of the opera is met with cheers from
the ragtag group, marking a victory for the hood.
Then began the movement,
a defense against the historic trend of displacement.
Not just in their city but others.
Connecting through hashtags and protests,
the fight to preserve minority communities is arduous.
Yet it grows, bringing understanding to the masses.
A city is individual, but the hood is collective
and it's not going anywhere.

BAHIA ZARATE

LA FRUTA DE TRABAJO

Roots dig into unfamiliar soil,
one it was never meant to know.
The intricate web spreads far and wide
in search of nutrients now found in pesticides.
Chemical intervention, because the growers can't
risk complying with Pachamama's limits,
feeding the roots toxins and urging it to produce
grapes, apples, strawberries, lettuce, tomatoes.
The produce isn't healthy, not with the toxins in the soil
pesticides on the plant. But that piece of knowledge
is forgotten in conversations about humane dietary restrictions.
Debates about animal cruelty discuss morality and knowing where
food is sourced, but forgotten is the group who picks it.
The farm workers reduced to a moment in history,
taught to have been resolved. A photo depicts an apple
freshly plucked from the tree. A symbol of manufactured freshness,
rests cradled in a hand, its red skin glistening in the sun.
The hand is a forgotten detail,
calloused and tan from hard work under a hot sun. In the fields,
white dust coats the farm workers' hands. The pesticides leave
speckled scarring and the loss of fingernails.
But the work doesn't stop. ICE raids and death only open spots
for another farm worker to fill. Forgotten and vulnerable, the farm
workers continue the essential labor that no one wants to do. Picking the
food for a country that ignores their existence.
Comfort comes at the price
of overlooking injustice, but ignorance is all too common
when you only see the fruit of *their* labor.

Bahia Zarate is a poet from California. She attended the
University of California, Riverside and graduated in 2024 with
a bachelor's degree in Creative Writing. She has a forthcoming
poem in the 62nd edition of the Mosaic Magazine. She will be
attending the University of Glasgow in September to work
toward her Master's degree in Media Studies.

DECOLONIZE THIS POEM

"Decolonization or Extinction" ~ Elena Gomez, The Red Nation

De-Columbus Day this poem.
America wasn't discovered and explored.
It was invaded and colonized.

First and foremost this poem would like to
acknowledge it was written on Tongva land
De-canonize Junípero Serra.
A saint he ain't.
The original people of Los Angeles needed to be
saved from the savagery of colonialism, NOT
from the imaginary flames of a hell
with which this "Apostle of California" threatened
them unless they leave their heathen ways for
those of civilized Christendom.

This poem views the world through the eyes
of the colonized whether they be those of Jews
and Anglo-Saxons under domination of Rome
in ancient times or those of the Indigenous
under that of the United States and Canada
or Palestinians under that of Israel today.

De-militarize this poem.
Like Dwight Eisenhower said,
"Every gun that is made, every warship launched,
every rocket fired signifies, in the final sense,
a theft from those who hunger and are not fed,
those who are cold and are not clothed."

De-propagandize this poem.
As Malcolm X warned, "If you aren't careful,
the media will have you hating the people
who are being oppressed and loving the people
who are doing the oppressing."

De-Thanksgiving Day this poem.
This poem does not forget that this country
was founded on the ideology of white supremacy,
widespread practice of African slavery
and a policy of genocide and land theft, *
that under the pipelines, skyscrapers, mines
and oil rigs lie the interred bones, sacred objects
and villages of the ancestors of the first
peoples of the Americas."

CARL STILWELL

De-colonize Mother Earth.
Liberate her
skies from carbon dioxide and methane emissions,
oceans from being capital's plastic junkyard,
coasts from oil tanker spills and deepwater drilling blowouts,
and sacred soil from industrial agriculture, toxic runoff,
pesticides, mining, deforestation and desertification.

This poem like the poet who wrote it and those who
hear and/or read it, are a part of nature, NOT
separate from it, and thus one strand in the web of life
currently threatened by the sixth mass extinction.

De-commodify this poem.
It has value even if it doesn't add one cent
to unlimited wealth accumulation of richest 1%

De-privatize this poem
and re-communalize it.
As Roque Dalton has said,
"Creo que el mundo es bello,
que la poesía es como el pan,
de todos."
"I believe the world is beautiful
and poetry, like bread,
is for everyone."

* *Roxanne Dunbar-Ortiz*

** *Kesha James, Red Nation Podcast, YouTube channel of the 55th annual National Day of Mourning protest in Plymouth, MA.*

Carl Stilwell is a retired teacher who taught for over 30 years in the Los Angeles Unified school District and participated in UTLA's teachers' strikes in 1970 and 1989. He was born during the depression in Oklahoma and came to California in 1959 and has lived here ever since. His pen name was inspired by the Joads struggle for survival In The Grapes of Wrath and the songs and life of Woody Guthrie. He has poems published in Altadena Poetry Review, Blue Collar Review, Four Feather's Press, Lummox, Pearl, Prism, Revolutionary Poets Brigade – Los Angeles, Rise Up, Sequoyah Cherokee River Journal, The Sparring Artists, and The New Verse News.

No Ticket

There is not a river of billionaire blood deep
or wide enough for me to shed a tear on its bank
I want to thank
The members of the bourgeoises
For making it so easy
To recruit thirsty shitposters
To the cause of radical redistribution
We're all learning there's no substitution
For extremely direct solutions
Privacy suddenly seems to mean something
To the ones who've been compulsively gathering
The collective metadata of the masses
Maybe this time we get off our asses it's only
Class war if we fight back
And everything is under attack
but maybe if we
Consciously
Take a minute to breathe
Invest in our community
It doesn't have to be
Rope a dope again
Return of the robber barons
Final solutions part two
Spare me your electric boogaloo
Tell the boys if they want to take the involuntary
Out of celibate
Find a worthy cause
And fight for it
Stop displacing onto
People who have as little or less than you
It starts
At the top
We all know what it takes
For the bleeding to stop
I'm no accelerationist I never asked to live in times like this
 but watch me match the speed of traffic
No ticket

Anna Geoffroy

TROLLEY PROBLEM

If you do nothing the girl tied to the train tracks dies
If you do nothing the saw mill cuts the girl in half
Snidely Whiplash twirls his mustache
If you do nothing five people are killed by the runaway trolley car

If you do nothing a billion people you don't know will die
And the price of food will keep going up

If you do nothing the cost of housing keeps rising while
The skylines are filled with empty investment apartments
The suburbs fall apart as services and bridges collapse
Sewers and gas lines make the worst of friends on tree-lined lanes

If you do nothing the man in the apartment dies
Because the only lever he has his hand on is whether
He buys his insulin or the food
That triggers his need for insulin

If you pull the lever one person dies
And you have to live with the consequences

If you do nothing the CEO authorizes implementation
Of the unfinished, untested, flawed and faulty algorithm
And gives a TED talk about having to crack a few eggs
(the opposite of anti-abortionists, he means people when he says eggs)

If you do nothing the hospital turns the woman having a miscarriage
Away from the ER for fear of lawsuit

If you do nothing the lawsuits keep happening
And state's rights suddenly revert to nobody's rights
Landowners rights, billionaire's rights, divine rights to rule
Neofeudalist protomonarchy ruthlessly enforcing white hegemony

If you do nothing the CEO tells the risk assessors
The cost of human life is set by the courts
And to make the best decision
For the shareholders

If you do nothing the numbers on the guillotine graph
Keep
Going
Up

If you do nothing the CEO buys another yacht
To house all the people who do all the work
On the much nicer yacht
Because they ruin the aesthetic

Someone is running around
Tying pretty girls
To trolley tracks

If you do nothing there will be another e-coli recall
Listeria recall
Salmonella recall
Trichinosis outbreak
Measles outbreak
Polio outbreak

If you do nothing your neighbor who got behind on their paperwork
Gets taken away in a van
And you never see them again

If you do nothing the CEO signs the paperwork
To build the pipeline
That causes the spill
That poisons the water
That poisons the well

If you do nothing there is another unanswered for cancer cluster
Another dustbowl another stock crash
Soup line redline mine collapse

If you do nothing the girls who died in Lowell won't be
The last ones
The radium girls won't be
The last ones
The matchstick girls won't be
The last ones
Are we
The last ones?

If you pull the lever the trolley
Runs over the man tying people to the railroad tracks

For legal reasons
This poem
Is about nothing

Anna Geoffroy is a Massachusetts-based poet, propagandist and pope (non-exclusive). She is the co-host of the live-to-tape Contro-Verse open mic in Malden and editor of the Holy Nonsense project. Together with fellow Garage Poets Jeff Taylor and Ethan Mackler she has performed at festivals, galleries, coffee shops and porch fests from Manchester to Lynn. Her work has been featured in the Lines Connecting Lines exhibit at UMA, the Malden Covid Memorial, The Blood Rag, and a street post near you.

THE DREAM

The dream is gone,
do you want another one?

No sun-born for me
no friends
no family
I'm just a shy – boy
sitting by the wall
always in a hurry,
inpatient dreamer of a dream

Mother, don't you hear
your baby's crying
Mother, all of your
baby – toys are broken

"Baby, take your first walk
out into the Waste – land"!

If there were water
and no rock
and if there were rocks
and also water
a spring
a pool amongst the rock
IF THERE WAS A SOUND OF WATER ONLY...

There is nothing that is real
nothing I can touch
I just don't feel

Now I know – the heaven is not for me.

Falling, falling
I can't see the bottom
but the things look a lot better
when they're seen from far away

GOOD BYE!
I'LL PROBABLY NEVER SEE YOU AGAIN!!!

Alen Nanov, born 1972 in Skopje Macedonia. His greatest passions since the last century are the theater, poetry, music, art... LIFE! "TO BE, A HUMAN HAS TO BE AN ARTIST"!!! is his moto!!!

I Am Speaking

after Kamala Harris

I am speaking my soul
into the yawning endless throat

of absence, an emptiness, a chasm gouged
brutal at the core of all things where,

hollow and hungry,
it guzzles each word.

I am speaking incantations
to ward off the ghosts

whose voices quake in the chest,
shatter the windows, draw the heart in

on itself so hard it becomes
a vicious gravity into which one

must never stop speaking:
a gravity which demands to be fed.

I am speaking now
because later, when it's dark,

they will speak. Piercing enough
to rent floors and earth, to tear breath from the lungs

of the living
who have spoken the way

I am speaking, now, to the children, alive –
those longing for a softness

they can't yet name;
new babies drawing first breaths

of grief and black air –
hush, hush, is what I say;

I am speaking now.
My voice is bombs.

Every tremor rocks them further
into quiet; into dark.

Felicia Krol

I will put them to sleep,
then keep speaking to drown out

their screams.
Hush, I'll speak, loud, to the night.

Hush now, child. My turn to speak.

Hush, child. Hush, child.
Hush, hush, hush.

To Plant a Garden in Gaza

is to kneel in the dirt of one's homeland,
besieged,
and speak new roots to the earth.

To stand in the shadow of death
and call life into being.

To lend one's thirst; to practice its quenching.
To be, together,
and be.

Why should such joy be met with wrath?
Why, then, should anyone ever again
anticipate grace? Or peace?

For Medo Halimy, 19 years old,
killed by an Israeli airstrike
after eleven months of
genocide.

Felicia Krol (she/her) is a writer and educator based in Detroit, Michigan, where she works as a Writer-in-Residence with InsideOut Literary Arts, bringing poetry into K-12 schools and celebrating youth voice and agency. Her fiction and poetry has appeared in various journals, including Hayden's Ferry Review, Mid-American Review, and Rattle.

STRUGGLE BUS REVOLUTION

Being in therapy has brought me to the realization
that I'm terrible at life.
I fumble across a spectrum of struggle buses
masking their way through rotary after rotary.

I'll never be the most reliable voice in your wallet
but I'll always be stretching the limits
of steel and rubber,
I'll always be discovering new methods
of driving my struggle bus.

When turning toward home
isn't on the checklist
when time is ten different things
that end in unpaid bills,

I'll be building tree forts at the rendezvous
waiting with a bong and a pocketful of second chances
sparking the kind of revolution
that inspires every cog in the wheel
to make therapy appointments.

We'll inhale and inhale
lighting small fire after small fire
until our personal tragedies
smolder to ash.
Holding the world in our lungs
a little too long
as we learn to breathe through the burning.
We release what's left in the smoke
back into the air
watching the struggles rebuild themselves in the wind.

Maybe this time I won't spill the bong
but don't hold your breath
I'm terrible at life. Jeff Taylor
Instant Karma Car Bomb

Someone looking televised
and vaguely clipboard

knocked at my car window
asking if they could scrub my language
while telling me my driving sucks.

Afraid my phonetics
have taken up wrestling
sounding more like turnbuckles and piledrivers
than consonants and vowels
I wrote everything I intended to say
like the judge's stenographer
taking notes in the dark.

Fire engine. Breakfast.
Is that a grenade or a lanyard?
Turn left. Violets. Try this for your diamonds
covered in violins and the silhouette
of a candlestick.

The frequency of formulation
caused me to pull the car over
the composition decomposing
into an interior monologue.

Angry hair. Pungent poignant.
Shifted dove canon. Driftwood pedestal.
Deviated handshake. Instant Karma Car Bomb.

Before I found the curb
the cameras were rolling
like they found their orbit.

When I was handed a script
I instinctively started reading
the double-spaced typed lines
as if I've been waiting years
for this moment to appear like a lost key.

I couldn't make out the words
but I knew I was expected to say something

so I told him what I thought he needed to hear
but maybe it was me who needed to hear it.

Pour kerosene on the comments section
burn the internet
charred and hollow
like the brick-and-mortar
of our wide eyes.

Let the flames train an Ai poet
to construct a romantic dirge
a found poem pieced together
on clipboards strewn across
the sidewalk of our insulted intelligence.

We'll all learn the words
it will be our common language
it will be our way home.

The late **Jeff Taylor** lived with his wife and kids in Malden, Massachusetts. He was one of the organizers of ControVerse Open Mic, and a member of the performance troupe The Garage Poets. Jeff's poems have appeared in journals and anthologies, including Tickets To Midnight Vol.3 (Pure Sleeze Press), GAS: Poetry, Art & Music, Ain't no Deadbeats Around Here, New Generation Beats Anthology 2023, EthelZine, American Graveyard Anthology, Unlikely Stories Mark V, Oddball Magazine, The Blood Shed Review, Cajun Mutt Press, The Blood Rag, Poetry Cove Magazine, and more. Depose was his final poetry submission.

A Gene for Tears

Even if you watch this country with the sound turned down, all the venom and hurt still bruise through. So many derangements arranged in strange and familiar ways.

Intoxicated logic. Unmended melodies with insufficient pills or winning streaks to take them across the finish line.

Even with the sound turned down, you can still hear a cry take hold in the throat.

You understand how a battered body knows its way around a twelve-bar blues when jagged howls of fist verbs shatter the air.

Even with the sound down, a down sound, you can still hear how some are beat so bad their spilled blood becomes jazz,

a music to hymn a broken body to heaven.

DEAR AMERICA,

Where are your papers to show your citizenship?
What are your thoughts on democracy?

America, your erogenous zones have become hot-button issues. Your
blood is poisoned with racism, radicalism, misinformation, and political
polarization.

America, stop melting down bullets to make crowns for your molars.
Stop building playgrounds for new Hitler youth.

And what about your thoughts on education? Can you read my letters
or calculate the difference between your richest and poorest citizens?

Dear America, is that a knife in your back? A ticking bomb beneath
your powdered wig? Your pork barrel politics are stuffed with
trichinosis. Your eyes have gone freedom blind.

Dear America, why haven't I heard back from you? Are you in prison?
If so, I'll send you a cake with a pen inside
      so you can write back.

L.A. poet/spoken-word performer **Rich Ferguson**
has shared the stage with Patti Smith, Wanda
Coleman, Moby, and other esteemed poets and
musicians. He is a featured performer in the
film, *What About Me?* featuring Michael Stipe,
Michael Franti, k.d. lang, and others. His poetry
and award-winning spoken-word music videos
have appeared in numerous anthologies and
festivals. Ferguson is the lead editor of an
anthology of CA poets entitled *Beat Not Beat* (Moon Tide Press). He was selected
by the National Beat Poetry Foundation, Inc. (NBPF), to serve as U.S. Beat Poet
Laureate (Sept. 2023 to Sept. 2024).

THE CAFE FASCIST

he's a fascist fountain
spurting out slaved words

not knowing he is salted
with the rich man's poison

one and one add up to lies
the press merely reporters

passing on the obvious truth
not Eton educated sycophants

tonguing their masters half
arsed versions of a world view

that only exists in focus groups
and the shopping lists of the rich

but still he spurts on into the ear
of an old man silent and battered

in a blue anorak and baseball cap
he nods along to the happy slaves

miserable twitter of painful song
he's a fascist fountain powered

by pain, loss, hatred, confusion,
and the need to parrot back any

kind of explanation in the absence
of a party who can make one & one

add up to more than ruling class
narrowed perspectives telling him

he is speaking what makes sense
when like a loyal dog he has mistaken

his master's voice for his own, and so
he sits here, white as a sheet, fully boned.

John G. Hall was founding editor of radical arts magazine Citizen32 & was political activist in the 1980's. Published in 'Emergency Verse' and 'The Robin Hood Book' edited by Alan Morrison. Also, in volumes 1,2 and 3 of 'Best of Manchester Poets' published by Puppywolf. His collection 'Poems for Explosion' is published by Crisis Chronicles Press Cleveland Ohio. His latest book 'Making the Dark Visible' is published by Some Roast Poets publications, Manchester UK. He runs the Manchester Beat poetry night 'Beatification'. For the past 10 years he has organised a writers' retreat on the Island of Arran, Scotland. He has a degree in English Literature & Creative Writing from the University of Salford.

NON SPEGNETE LE LUCI

Il vento
sfacciato
strattona
il lavoro sconfitto
e
la sua dispersa
epopea

Lo scardinamento
lo sberleffo
rottamatore
nell'artefatta
naturalezza
riverbera
spergiudicati
devastanti
squarci
d'animalita'
padronale

Nel cimitero d'occidente
la farfalla ateniese
e'
una nebulosa
capace di
riscattare
le rovine
delle storie
la disfatta
sui piu' poveri
ormai
scorie
del tempo
del sentimento
dell'esecuzione
dell'economia
Leggere Marx con una mano sola
l'altra e' imbrattata
di merda
di sangue
con farciture
pubblicitarie
nel cielo
stellato
del capitale

SANDRO SARDELLA

E' necessario
in questo senso di
annientamento
tradire le consegne
mostrandone le
nudita'
cercare
la lezione
clandestina
contro
il potere

Unita' & frammenti
incandescenza & e lotte
dopo & oltre
l'ingombro
della deriva
come scavando
nel sottosuolo
disseminare
raccogliere
bruciare
bruciarsi
in rotture & saldature
corpo che diventa anima
anima che torna corpo
in una disperata & sperata
danza

Nelle luci del mattino
tra le nuvole
del mutevole cielo
di Milano
galleggia
il profumo
degli amori
clandestini
volano
migliaia di
fogli di carta
colorati
volano & parlano
fragili
duri
teneri
disperati
di
tre uomini soli
in cima
alla torre
di una fabbrica

Non spegnete le luci.

DON'T TURN OFF THE LIGHTS

The insolent
wind
tugs
the defeated work
and its lost
epopee

The unhinging
the demolishing
sneer
of artificial
naturalness
reflects the
unbiased
devastating
bestial
mastership
gashes

In the western cemetery
the athenian butterfly
is a nebula
able to
release
history's
ruins
the debacle
of the poorest
by now
scum
of time
of feeling
of execution
of economy

Reading Marx with one hand
the other one is dirty
with shit
with blood
with advertising
stuffing
among the capital's
starry
sky

Within this sense
of annihilation
it's necessary to
cheat on deadlines
disclosing their
nudities
looking for the
undercover
lesson
against
power

Unity & fragments
incandescence & battles
after & beyond
the destruction
of deviation
like digging
through the underground
scattering
harvesting
burning
getting burned

in damage and burning
the body turning into soul
the soul going back to body
in a desperate and awaited
dance

In the morning lights
among the cloud
of Milan's
variable sky
floats
the smell
of clandestine loves
thousand
colored
sheets of paper
fly
fly and speak
fragile
though
tender
desperate
to three lonely men
on top
at a factory's
tower

Don't turn off the lights.

(Translation from Italian by Jack Hirschman and Giovanni Romano)

 **Sandro Sardella** is a poet and painter from Varese in Northen Italy. His poetics are innervated by the experience of factory work and the political and avant-garde movements of the 1960/70s. Jack Hirschman translated and published his poems. He red at the 2012 San Francisco International Poetry Festival. In 2022 he red at the Elba Poetry Festival organized by Mark Lipman and in 2024 he red in Campi Bisenzio/Firenze at the 2° Literature Working Class Festival.

Sandro Sardella è poeta e pittore nato a Varese nel nord Italia. La sua poetica è innervata dall'esperienza del lavoro in fabbrica e dai movimenti politici e le avanguardie degli anni 1960/70. È stato più volte tradotto e pubblicato da Jack Hirschman che nel 2012 lo invitò all'International Poetry Festival in San Francisco. Ha partecipato invitato da Mark Lipman all'Elba Poetry Festival nel 2022 e nel 2024 è stato invitato al 2° Festival di Letteratura Working Class a Campi Bisenzio/Firenze.

Zen Poem for Peace

Some folks still live in the memories of their homes, floods, hurricanes, quakes, volcanoes, insecurity, disorientation, panic, and confusion.

They look at the wars and air their views about what they breathe, see, hear, and feel because they are still alive. The view of life can be

shaped by truth. People need lands of love to create new citizenries; bright tracer fires of the wars and the red of Aurora on the sky can redden

the snow, the trees, the moon; blood and sufferings; hearts; to bless and to sprinkle holy water; expiation and inspiration.

to harm life for the purpose of conquering the whole world; getting nowt; to own something that no longer exists or to be a symphonic poem,

a dwelling place for words needing interconnectedness to enhance understandings; telltales sighs of love; loaves belonging to an otherworldly

dimension; God, the gift; folks like pink sandcastles or like age-old allegories undergoing the Renaissance; all are born to run into their shadows.

To be buried in order to become living worms; a part of us; not useful; missing words; living words that grow up and multiply; memories.

Marieta Maglas lives in France. The Oddville Press, Sybaritic Press, Prolific Press, Silver Birch Press, Lothlorien Poetry Journal, Dashboard Horus, Al-Khemia Poetica Journal, Southern Arizona Press, Akita International Haiku Journal, The Queer Gaze, PentaCat Press, Coin-Operated Press, Mayari Literature, and others have published her poems. She's the author of Eschatological Regression and Cubic Words. She is a World Poetry Canada nominee, in 2013. She co-authors some anthologies like Near Kin: A Collection of Words and Art Inspired by Octavia Estelle Butler, The Cardinal Anthology Vol. 3, and Ain't no Deadbeats Around Here.

PARDON THE INTERRUPTION

Pardon the interruption,
Urgent message encoded
Must incite right to write,
Must not be malevolent but benevolent
Belly up, chin scrapes upper-crusted skies
Urgent message encoded
News media commits subterfuge through clip prisms
Pardon the interruption,
There seems to be delays in our systems,
Crash, system, system, crash, wipe, being hacked
Bandits besiege newsrooms, editors, interns take shelter
Warning signs need be heeded,
violence can outbreak as viruses do
Pardon the interruption,
Distended arms raised, sweat glands catalyzed
by feverish nerves codify situations
Outlaws compromising institutions of power,
a mad scramble, everyman for himself
Urgent message encoded, looting and pillaging
Death by dirty deeds, citizens with checkered pasts,
mannerisms, gaits of chimpanzees
Crust in eyes, plot against America,
externalized ambitions from within
Topple of power structures, structural damage to foundations
Finagle switches, shock to schemes, building blueprints burned
Cinder and ash, fires of worth formerly stoked, crowded canvas
Urgent message encoded
Intake nutrition you breathe, protect loved ones,
adoration earned not extorted
Pardon the interruption
Gas leak in interiors, underground bunkers buckle us down,
we hunker as bombs increase blast radiuses
Mushroom clouds contain cyanide,
poisonous to organs, optics affected
Please, pardon the interruption
No more messages ably broadcast

DOUGLAS CALA

TAKING THE VICTORS TO TASK

Light the candle,
Splintering of conscience
A meeting adjourns
Able minded warriors utilize their skills
Muscled by the God's

They, in lockstep with the rhythms of conformity
Lies espoused from tongues too coarse for cohesive speech

Satellites installed by super conglomerates
Spy on society
Frontiers of evolution have amounted to this!
A new technological arms race
Speeches to save face do no courtesy
Stifled by corruption
We need a reduction in rampant injustice

Laced by rhapsody
They think if you sing it it'll be a little more palatable
Purgatory probes
Can we galvanize hope, in force,
to act as a lure for better tomorrows?
Waves of tepid oceanic filth clog a once clear shoreline
Agricultural abundance once deterred the abominable

We are all bearing witness to a new age of man
A sinister web of name calling and self-aggrandizement
that even cosmetic surgery can't obscure
It is time to take the victors to task

Douglas G. Cala is a spoken word performance poet, editor, essayist, and multimedia/IT specialist from New York City. He has been published in a wide range of anthologies and printed journals both nationally and internationally. When not writing and reciting, Douglas works full time for NYC Public Schools' Division of Instructional Information Technology as an IT Support Specialist. You may learn more about him and his work by visiting his *Poets & Writers* directory profile.

TO PUT DOWN

"We are servers, not servants."
~ Mary Ann M. (1928 - 1986)

That silent December morning
the sky broke open, snowflakes
the size of butterflies dropped
on her mourners huddled in a tent.

At the visitation the night before
the restauranteur of white tablecloths
and Lithuanian duck had sent
flowers arranged in a tea service
for her head waitress, the shop steward.
"Bitch, it's her night off"
was not screamed as the visiting
second assistant pastor mingled
among the remains of the family.

That father who had raised me once said
it was good to think of college
get a job where you didn't
wear a uniform or work with your hands.
Respect. People had a right
to look down on me; I didn't
finish high school.
No – I pushed back at the 62-year-old
who had walked the USW strike line
every other day for two years
to keep retiree health care and pensions.
The company then sold and resold
pensions passed to a failing government agency
and retiree healthcare policies stopped
a month after his own death.

The flag of the dignity of work
gets raised as a distraction from
the indignity of teetering on the edge
of the maw of wage disparity and
unsafe working conditions
no fair funding for higher education
or trade schools, the redlining
of small business capital.
We demand to work with dignity.

ELIZABETH MARINO

Certification: *This poem was not written by a replicant.*
This poet worker reserves the right to be fully human
and sourced from proud people of hue. ###

Elizabeth Marino is a Chicago poet, performer, and
educator. A Pushcart Prize nominee, her work
includes: the full-length hybrid poetry/memoir
Asylum (Vagabond, 2020); the chapbooks Debris
(Puddin'head Press) and Ceremonies (dancing girl
press); over 20 print anthology contributions; and
various litzines.

DENNIS

Well worn beneath his tousled
Tufts of sparse, ancient hair
Dennis drags off the cigarette
and sets his triangle square

He hacks back the threatening
Death in his tar, blackened lungs.
The rains will soon be bringing the
Seasonal end; He holds the stud plum.

His arthritic fingers, curled over with age
And experience, lament other places
He could have, should have, been by now..
His pencil runs the straight edge traces.

This underbid job will not pay the rent,
So he ponders his word selection,
In adjusting the costs to his client.
Run the tape and work the calculations.

Slam! Slam! The hammer drives the nail.
His wife requires new medical treatments
And the insurance premiums must prevail.
Post set to vertical, he pours the mixed cement.

The time bomb that is his beat up pick-up truck,
Tires worn thin, topped with rusted ladder rack;
It has tallied up 259,000 miles on borrowed luck,
– Hired day laborers unload the bed from its back.

Screw -and saw -and drive -and drill!
Autumn is closing down, like the options of his life.
With the job up next, perhaps he can squirrel
Away enough comfort to surpass another winter's bite?

Thoughts weigh heavy in his gallimaufry of mental clutter,

As he hacks back death in his tar, blackened lungs.
Padding about his Pendleton pockets, searching for his lighter,
As he sets the length of lumber and holds the stud plum.

Dig Men! Dig!

The rains are coming! Dig Men! Dig!
Shore up those sieving gaps, and cracks of plaster
Store thy reserves squirrel!
Or you shall have no bread...

Burden your back and sweat of thy brow.
Prepare! Prepare! Prepare!
And for the love of Christ, man,
Do not fritter! Time lost is a precious resource,
Never to again be recovered.

So hear me when I, in earnest, say unto you:
Be not a Charity Case left in the bitter winter cold.
Dig Men! Dig! Strain and flex knotted muscle,
And concern yourself not with matters of frivolity.

Such as Pontificatious Poetry.....

Mark Novak is a poet who writes primarily from the San Francisco Bay Area. He holds an M.A. in Creative Writing and Poetry from San Francisco State University. His work has been seen in the Lothlorien Journal of Poetry, the Monterey Poetry Review, the Bards West Anthology, and the Cocktales literary of DearBooze.com. His work, 'The Vagabond Quothe Shakespeare' was the 6th place finalist in the Writer's Digest North American Poetry Awards (2017). His manuscript Sonnets For Agnodice was a winning selection in Finishing Line Press' 2025 Open Chapbook Contest and was published by FLP. Mark is both a regularly contributing writer and voice talent for readings with the poetry site Voetica.com.

The Workers on Land

There was a time in a very distant past
In the wilderness frisking men in amassed
Galloping through the dense green over the verdant plains
Picking golden nuts and berries to store before the long incoming rain

Men or even women hunt the wild for meat or for their skin
Hunting and gathering encapsulated
simply the labor into the vast land
Life's in prosperity where buds and fledglings
continuously birthed from the fertile ground
Wind made changes to the land
from a million folds and lifts across time

Stonewalls rise above the Earth and engine
starts to roar at the sky
Men start to wear in sleeves and industry
has replaced the primitive in alternate
Under the beam of light, labor enclosed
from the shade of the sun
Scribble by pen and machines clicking
instead of tools which are carved out from stones

Time may differ on how efforts are done
but they both still meet to thrive
Feet stride before through the long bushes
and across the thick woods
Through the pavement road
and inside the cemented walls and floors will now enter
Both different in sight but akin anticipating
for some privilege and bounty there maybe awaiting

Hands can be toiled from the hard labor it may seems
Constant drive that rarely bends hoping in return for some rich gain
Mishaps arrive when the opportunities on land regress
or when resources decline
Where must these hands need to till
when only debts and troubles left even for scavenging

Carlos Guinita

A LABOR'S TALE

Along the thick pages of history
Good men have always been working for order and civility
The fertile land that is tilled for food
Houses with huge chimneys
to reshape the bounds of land and sea
Walls and roads mined from the tallest mountain
Treasure beneath the ground
that lighted out households and buildings
Proud labor has showered men
with comfort in different forms and numbers
From the brightest mind where ideas are born
And the hands that molds and crafts with ingenuity
Society has flourished with the ample bounty of the Earth
Daily job may be deemed of story twisted
with boredom and without glory
But the hand that moves with long familiarity of hard labor
And to which fingertips bounded to its extension
along with companionship
Never a burden to a worker
who just known the everyday rhythm of service
In exchange for the mind and body's labor,
should one be compensated
Wage is gold for the laborer to buy his own necessity
For the body to continuously work,
the mind should always be fed
A more help it can do when it can feed a family or two
After one hard day,
little success has been shared across the hallway
Hardworking men leaving the premises
and another memory in gay
Errors or even one rigorous task can bear the persistent
But cannot withstand the struggle along with a sudden halt
The hand has reached the edges of his long and endurable effort
Where its labors and pains may seem to run short
Another tale of the fate of a hardworking man
added to the rich pages of history

Carlo R. Guinita is a license Agricultural Engineer by profession. He is a Filipino and currently residing at Digos City, Davao del Sur. He published a research article posted at Academia and Marine Agronomy website entitled "Growth of Carrots Supplied with Different Levels of Kappaphycus alvarezii drippings Delivered through Subsurface Drip Irrigation under Greenhouse Structure." He reviewed a research paper publish at Vietnam Journal for Agricultural Sciences. His first poetry pieces were accepted at Poet But Us. He writes as his hobby and passion.

SHADOWS AT DAWN

The bus groans awake like the rest of us,
silence surrounds the few cars
traveling the streets this hour.
I glance around at the faces beside me,
they appear as worn as mine.
Trapped in the repeated cycle of shadows,
work, sleep, and repeat, day in and day out.

It is cold outside; my breath fogs the window
My hands tremble from the chill,
Outside of the bus, life appears blurred,
The glow from the streetlights nearly vanished
In the last moments of night, when darkness
fades into dawn. This is my life, years of struggling,
of hard work for the promises made to my family.

The bus jolts across the unkept road,
a man in the next row is jostled from sleep.
His head nods in desperation for a moment of rest.
A woman holds her coffee tightly to prevent it from spilling
She catches my eye. We stare at one another, I nod.
She nods back, understanding each other's burden
We are on this journey together, our quiet,
unspoken pact of surviving.

Glancing out the window, I think of my children
Their breaths rise and fall inside their dreams
while I work and grind to turn the hours into bread
Into rent, into hope for a better future.
The bus jolts again against the broken road
as the hum of the engine mumbles.
I pull the yellow stop request cord.
Stepping off the bus, I know the day will engulf my entirety,
And swallow me as I work with tired hands and an aging body.

I do this for my wife and my children,
hoping that I can provide a better life for them
so that they do not have to work as I do.
So that they do not have to leave their children
While they dream.
Knowing that I am not alone.
We are not alone.

JACALYN EYVONNE

BREAK ROOM CONFESSIONS

Reheated leftovers fill the air
as the microwave hums in the background.
The breakroom slowly comes to life.
Smells of hot coffee, two-day-old pasta,
last night's fried chicken,
floating beneath overly bright fluorescent lights
flickering overhead.
Tired bodies move slowly as they enter the breakroom,
gravitating to their usual places, chairs without names,
but remembered by the room of varying personalities,
each weary from work, but each respectful
of one another and our collective resilience.

Jennifer unwraps a sandwich, sharing stories
about her kids between each bite.
Michael unlaces his boots, kicking them off.
'My feet feel like they're on fire."
"I know the feeling," someone remarks,
"I soak my feet every night."
"Yeah, another day, another hard dollar," Michael sighs.
Javier bursts out with another unfunny joke.
His jokes never make sense, but the room laughs anyway.
Tears stream down the faces of some as though
their laughter was stuck inside, fighting to be set free –
released from the stress that engulfs them.
Offering a bit of joy for the remaining fifteen minutes
spent together.
The laughter makes each one of us feel better,
notwithstanding the arduous work that awaits.

Some announce their plans for the weekend,
a few quietly complain about management,
while others share their dreams.
Michael plans to purchase a new car.
Susie's desire to buy a new house,
Johnathan dreams of opening a small restaurant.
Bound together in a room of smells and hums
as time races to rush us back to the floor
where rows of monotony drive us like robots
alongside machines that make us feel
less human in our repetitiveness.
Yet, inside this comfort room,
in the space of the minutes together,
we share our hopes and dreams,
where we become comedians and storytellers,
exhausted together but stubborn in shared hope.

The clock ticks, the smells linger,
as the spell of joy is broken and we rise
to return to the cold machinery awaiting,
optimistic for the shared camaraderie
that we will find once again, in the breakroom
the following day.

 **Jacalyn Eyvonne** Poet Laureate, Vallejo, CA. (01/01/2024-
12/31/2025) is the author of *I Am Not An Inconsequential
Word, Venting To Verse-How To Turn Anger Into Poetry*, and
*The Unyielding Weight of Words-Poems on Reflection,
Healing, and Love.* Her poem *Where Sand, Sea, and Dreams
Collide*: appears on the joint project of the California Poet
Laureate and California Arts Council "Our California"
project. Published work includes Oakland Tribune,
Wheelsong Poetry 3&4, United Kingdom; Hues of Spring
Anthology, Nyra Publishers; World Healing Peace, Inner
Child Press International; editor, Youth Poetry Letters –
Pencils and Dreams, and others. Former founder /
publisher *In The Company of Poets* Magazine, and current director of
Monologues and Poetry International Film-Fest. Jacalyn is an Academy of Art
University SF graduate in Motion Picture and Television.

MOURNING

There is no time to mourn
the rich and powerful
with their millionaire salaries
and their putrid practices
and their useless meetings

I mourn the babies in Palestine
dying of hunger, dying of cold,
dying unnatural deaths –
brought to you by the
empire that knows no honor nor shame

I will mourn those who die
an unnatural death every day –
there is nothing natural about greed,
there is nothing natural about empire –
everything will fall

hopefully not with us inside.

MY MAMA TAUGHT ME SOLIDARITY

Every now and then,
someone would knock at our door,
asking for a leaf, or a branch
of one of my mama's plants,
she would never say no,
and never accepted payment

When I was little, she would
always tell me to be of use,
to help when possible,
to not be a coward who
puts his head down at the
sound of anyone's voice

Sometimes I'd scare her
with my political activities,
but I'd tell her she was to blame,
and she'd look at me with
the death stare only a loving
mother knows

I am not my mother's
wildest dream, I hope I am
her joy, and her anger, and her
frustration and her creativity
and her madness, and her love –
I am her and she is me.

Jesus Cortez is a writer, poet and photographer from West Anaheim. Through his artistic expressions, he brings forth counter narratives to those presented in the mainstream. In addition, he hopes to use his voice in contrast to those who tend to speak for his community. His work has appeared in Harvard Palabritas, the Acentos Review, Contrapuntos X Oeste, Drifter Zine, WAYF Journal and Tule Review, among other publications.

WE'RE COOKING
AND WE'RE NOT EVEN CHEFS

enough of this and you cure the longing
enough of this and you can find yourself
building mountains out of piles of dust
building meaning from the endless despair
but with this we are not broken
we are constellations of trauma and loss
we are cogs in a sinister corporate machine
we are doing just fine until the drugs are gone
but even swan songs have gentle melodies
so we hum and we laugh and stumble over the words
like it's not the only damned tune we know

we live by the golden rules of the ones before us
what goes on in the room stays in the room
and you're not a junkie if you're wearing your work boots
and that the counter in the closet isn't for eating
but for following lines to their own conclusions
just like we're doing, following each balloon to heaven

in the blood on the floor. our reflections
paint scarlet vignettes of better men
who greet each morning clean and innocent
praying to their twelve-step totems
but that life was never meant for men like us
we were born to drink our pain from the work nights
to climb out of the gutter where we were born
to make the whole damn neighborhood proud
to greet each morning with our heads above our hauntings

the real truth is something that can't be spoken
the sins of our fathers are scarred on our souls
we built ourselves from the ruins of other men's dreams
you can clean up your act but your eyes carry the burden
and ours hold the stories that only come out at night
when the party's over and our work boots are off
and the liquor outweighs our reservations
at twilight is when the dogs come out of the men
and we can curse the heavens and tilt our hats
to hell, and the silence that befalls us says it all

Damian Rucci a touring poet from New Jersey and the author
of nine books of poetry. He's the founder of the NJ Poetry
Renaissance and focus of the PBS documentary Voices in The
Garden. Damian has spent the last ten years bouncing around
the country performing in universities, bookstores, dive bars,
basements, and tattoo parlors. He's the founder of ten poetry
series including Puff Puff Poems and Poems & Punchlines.

Airplanes Anymore

He doesn't believe in airplanes anymore
The forces of flight, aflame in the night
Or in the way jet engines roar
All allure and mystery, misplaced in a helmet bag
Left on a ready-room floor, last century

Wedding bells and claxons
Toll over Albuquerque Central
Air control hyperbole
Let eagles and angels
Soar into infinity like flying monkeys

As he tapes his nylon
Sleeping tent back together
In the morning

So ground-bound, the sky itself
Can disappear
Without a warning

CLICHÉ

criminal to
outlaw to
counter culture to
pop culture to
cliché

And here it comes again

desperation to
life line to
opportunity to
choice to
option

feel free to disagree

counterpoints to
arguments to
fist a cuffs to
prison cells to
lawsuits

you have the right to all obscenity

criminal to
outlaw to
counterculture to
pop culture to
cliche

PW Covington is the NBPF's New Mexico Poet Laureate (2024-2026). Covington has spent decades traveling the highways of North America, sharing his poetry and prose. With numerous Best of the Net and Pushcart nominations, PW has been invited to share his work from Woodstock, NY to The Beat Museum in San Francisco. In 2019, his collection of flash fiction 'North Beach and Other Stories' was selected as a Finalist in LGBTQ+ Fiction by the International Book Awards. PW lives just south pf Historic Route 66, in Albuquerque, New Mexico, where he has worked on film and television projects including 'Better Call Saul'.

MOLTITUDINI

distopiche

serie televisive fra la federa e il cuscino
dadi di tofu al primo giro di revenge porn

ed un abbonamento di emozioni in differita
– con i pensieri assorti
sulle consegne a domicilio *Just Eat*

nel coprifuoco infrasettimanale
del canale DAZN.

cani da guardia in seconda serata
per chi si illude che un Serenase
allunghi la notte

<<E non è vero ciò che è vero
è vero ciò che *x.com*>>

dove un Magnesium tira l'altro

ma chi non Supradyn
non mangia.

I.

negli hashtag suburbani digitati col caps lock
contestazioni lunghe il tempo
di un'eterna adolescenza

sulle web radio proletarie
criptate in 5G
<<tumulti working class
a 6 cent. al minuto!>>

– un *laissez-faire* sintonizzato con i reels
per il settore giovanile
dell'alternanza scuola-lavoro

mentre i nativi digitali fanno i riti di iniziazione
e imparano a disabilitare
le finestre di pop-up.

i.

NELLE BATTAGLIE PER LO IUS SOLI
ALLE COPPIE DI FATTO SU BADOO

SFILANO FIGLIE ADOTTIVE
DEPOSITATE ALLA SIAE

II.

corsi di yoga sullo streaming della Soka Gakkai
e i caroselli con le breaking news
accessoriati nello screensaver

– gli incensi alla vaniglia ancora addormentati
sotto l'abat-jour

nei mantra mattutini
per i proseliti di StreamYard.

i.

bombardamenti a tappeto
dai call center di Vodafone Romania
ed un rifugio antiaereo
fra i contatti segnati come spam

– gli 007 dietro i banner con le pubblicità di Apple
o di Samsung S10

il controspionaggio fra l'informativa per la privacy
e le preferenze per i cookie.

MULTITUDES
dystopian

television series between the pillowcase and the pillow
tofu dice in the first round of revenge porn

and a subscription of deferred emotions
– with absorbed thoughts
on *Just Eat* home deliveries

during the midweek curfew
of the DAZN channel.

watchdogs in the late evening
for those who delude themselves that a Serenase
you extend the night

<<And what is true is not true
it's true what *x.com*>>

where one Magnesium leads to another

but who does not Supradyn
doesn't eat.

I.

in suburban hashtags typed with caps lock
long-lasting disputes
of an eternal adolescence

on proletarian web radios
encrypted in 5G
<<working class riots
at 6 cents. per minute!>>

– a *laissez-faire* tuned to the reels
for the youth sector
of school-work alternation

while digital natives perform initiation rites
and learn to disable
pop-up windows.

i.

IN THE BATTLES FOR IUS SOLI
TO ACTUAL COUPLES ON BADOO

ADOPTED DAUGHTERS PARADE
FILED WITH SIAE

II.

yoga classes on Soka Gakkai streaming
and carousels with breaking news
accessorized in the screensaver

– the vanilla incense still asleep
under the lampshade

in morning mantras
for StreamYard converts.

i.

carpet bombings
from Vodafone Romania call centers
and an air raid shelter
among contacts marked as spam

– the 007 behind the banners with Apple advertisements
or Samsung S10

counter-espionage between the privacy policy
and cookie preferences.

Edoardo Olmi was born in Florence in 1984. He published *Il porcospino in pegaso* ("The Porcupine into Pegasus", 2010), *R: exist-stance* (2017), *Stagioni scalene* ("Scalene seasons", 2021) and the anthological collection *Poesie scelte (2003-2021)* ("Selected poems (2003-2021)", 2023). He won the third prize of the Carver, the Nabokov Prize, the Il Delfino Prize and was a finalist in the fifth edition of the Prato Poesia Prize. His texts have appeared – among others – on the blogs of *La macchina sognante*, *Inverso*, *El Ghibli* and *Poesia del nostro tempo*. They have been translated into English for the magazines *Solstice*, *The Antonym* and for *Neke, The New Zealand Journal of Translation Studies* of the Victoria University of Wellington in New Zealand and in Romanian for the *Tribuna* magazine. He is currently the editor, together with Marco Incardona, of the Affluenti editorial series for Edizioni Ensemble.

Edoardo Olmi è nato a Firenze nel 1984. Ha pubblicato *Il porcospino in pegaso* (2010), *R: exist-stance* (2017), *Stagioni scalene* (2021) e la raccolta antologica *Poesie scelte (2003-2021)* (2023). Ha vinto il terzo premio del *Carver*, il *Premio Nabokov*, il *Premio Il Delfino* ed è stato finalista della V edizione del *Premio Prato Poesia*. Suoi testi sono apparsi – fra gli altri – sui blog de *La macchina sognante*, *Inverso*, *El Ghibli* e *Poesia del nostro tempo*. Sono stati tradotti in inglese per le riviste *Solstice*, *The Antonym* e per *Neke, The New Zealand Journal of Translation Studies* della Victoria University di Wellington in Nuova Zelanda e in rumeno per la rivista *Tribuna*. Attualmente è curatore, assieme a Marco Incardona, della collana editoriale di Affluenti per Edizioni Ensemble.

WHIMPER

Mine's a generation
of youth-worshippers
playing Fight Club
with middle age.
Hidden and haunted,
we work to find a way
through our anger
and make peace
with our lives
or adopt the mantra
"I deserved more,"
and drown the disappointment
in apathy, dollars or hate.

So welcome to Gen X, y'all,
the shit-show generation,
bottle fed fear of the bomb
mixed with neutral neglect.
Armed with MTV attention spans
and mad latch-key skills.
Raised with the push
to "be more"
in a repressed
50's kinda way.

We're the pickpocket gen
who found our truths
in rockers and peers,
lifted individuality
from the 60's
and stole our values from
Madonna and John Hughs.
We are the recipients of
trickle-down theory,
economics, trauma and pain.
So don't talk to strangers.
Don't ask and don't tell.
Suck it up and keep going,
because boys will be boys
and that's just how it is
if you're gay or a girl.

We are overachieving
"you can have it all"
Dance Moms and Soccer Dads.
We are plastic
"love is all the things"
because time equals money
and the lines became blurred.
We are wine with friends
and complaining
that they never come home
while we laugh about Glory Days
and wonder if a "side dick" or "chick"
would make us feel
just a little less alone.

We are the lost and the lonely
still trying to figure out
who the fuck we are,
ignoring the mess
the greatest gen left
and an environment the boomers
forgot they wanted to save.
We became or raised
the monsters hiding under the bed
and the only legacy we'll leave
is Kurt Cobain, more debt
and hollow, self-centered greed.

And if Ginsberg's
Beat generation
cried out
with a HOWL,
then this is the sound
of generation X
standing in the back
with a whimper.

ANXIETY

Daily, the world tilts more on a head
it shoves further up its own ass
while they condition us to just smile and swallow
whatever bullshit emerges from either end.

We're conditioned to follow, never to lead.
To be passive without the will to object.
To never question bestowed authority, saying,
"We don't need to understand."

The anxiety spreads, a virus passed
person to person, nerve cell by nerve,
but we're conditioned to ignore our knowing
that's telling us to sound the goddamn alarm.

To forget knees weren't made for bending
just because they tell us to kneel.
To accept the freedom we're given
at the cost of a voice they refuse to hear.

We live in the heart of darkness
and accept it as the light of the world.
while our forced docility is killing us
one overdosed youth at a time.

We need therapy to believe the shit is roses
and medicate our instincts so we can placidly comply.
We tell ourselves this is all normal,
but this is how the soul of a people dies.

Chris Dean, Indiana Beat Poet Laureate (2025-2027) is a storyteller, graphic designer and Magpie Poet who writes from the heart of Indiana where they live with their husband and too many cats to mention. They are the co-founder and managing editor of Keeping the Flame Alive Press. Their work has been featured online, in multiple print anthologies and they are the author of three full length books of poetry, "tales from a broken girl," "we're all stories in the end," and "pyre."

SOLIDARITY

Arise!
Arise for a better world not wilted from birth
free of famished bodies;
free of famished hearts,
we are labouring hard yet
crying out for tiny wages
with beads
of sweat on jagged heads
 trickling on tired faces,
but still, we rise, not rubbed out for a better tomorrow,
We rise across the fields
positive and bold.
Our spirits won't fold or burn
We rise holding hands,
holding our labouring arms and limbs
swaying in circles
within the strong breath of toil worse than a pandemic.
The capitalist arms circle our throats
then, we stop all the machines
and shut down offices-
Together we rise,
We rise,
to dismantle injustice inward and outward like
taking down a huge tired cake.
We rise,
we rise.
Together we rise as one!

AYO AYOOLA-AMALE

WORKING CLASS POWER

We toil for bread
till darkness whispers through the trees
yet, we get no right,
only heavy shocks
we work, we work
and toil till the dark comes down
crushing
the steel,
crushing the flour
and all the mills, all the offices
we labour dragged down-
it is still hard to believe that
our sweat, our bones, our blood,
fade off into a feathery shadow
fatigued and worn out,
With heads heavy and sore,
through the endless work.
Our cause is just,
our common bond-
the larger lights like a sky smiling
our hearts of valour
will STOP the power of capital
for "injury to one is an injury to all."
We cannot be stopped
fighting for our humanity.
Our Solidarity is forever!

Ayo Ayoola-Amale is a Creative director, author,
Performance poet, visual and mime artist. She is a
multiple award-winning peacebuilder, and poet
committed to Artistic Activism and lifting the
essential role of creativity in peace-building and
conflict transformation.

ACCIDENT AT THE MILL

for Ken Cathers

Ant
large in size,
a new friend
found in the sticks,
sticks going into stacks,
stacks of two by this
and two by that,
destined for the kiln.

Ant,
fallen between boards,
able to survive
a journey to me,
unprepared for the injury
you managed to take on,
your head up proud
but your rear-end taken.

Ant,
I see your legs
trying to do what
they always do,
carrying something,
but this moment
must be uncommon
as I see
and don't want to.

There is a different direction
you didn't choose
going in circle after circle,
all that can be
leaving me
the big reckless man,
trying to help those legs,
legs part of your damage,
part of how
any escape is possible.

Ant,
I don't give up.
I continue with a sliver
of fir, holding it so still,
moving it under
the crushed section

CHAD NORMAN

until I pick you up
and try to prevent
any further confusion.

Ant,
perhaps during the next shift
I will know
you survived,
see no sign of you
on any piece of wood.

INJUSTICE

As the good husband
    decides to wake
    and walk his son
    up a street
    to a good school,
    he decides to stare
    through what would be
    another morning,
    another bit of light
    his eyes allow to be
    what provides a new
    form of thinking,
    a new form of dealing
    with other men,
    men he must tolerate,
    men he must follow
    and they are not worth
    following,
    men at the job
    he rises to go to.

After a lunch is packed,
a wife kissed goodbye,
he prepares to become
what and who he must
pretend to be,
the worker, the factory boy,
someone his employer
insists on including
in a list of other men
they have lied to,
they have mismanaged,
they have taken money from,
they have chosen
to cheat families with
for some reason.

He knows they believe
he doesn't know.

The factory is wrong,
    the factory is unfortunate,
    being led by dysfunction,
    small men with big bellies,
    led by nothing other than
    small visions they see

CHAD NORMAN

when sitting in a bathroom,
or perhaps discussing
on a morning when they
know they will need
to lie, and look like
the honest guy
who says,
"My door is always open."

Casa Harris
April 28, 2010

Chad Norman from Nova Scotia in 1992 won the
Gwendolyn MacEwen Memorial Award For Poetry. His
new book, *A Life Between The Brackets*, is out Winter
2025/26 with Shadow Script Publishing (Ireland). His
poem, *The Shoulds*, in the *Lunar Vagabond Collection*,
went to the moon Feb. 26, 2025.

A WHOLE NEW FORMULA

Early in the morning in the office lot
It's hard to find a parking spot
The woman in her vehicle to the right
Is still covered in her blanket from the night

Homelessness in Northern California
Has a whole new formula
Not just low-income folks
The middle-class workers
Have nowhere to hang their coats

In front of me sleeping in the Camry
There is a whole family
And in the vehicle to my left
A trucker is having breakfast

Homelessness in Northern California
Has a whole new formula
Not just low-income folks
The middle-class workers
Have nowhere to hang their coats

It makes perfect sense
Because it's thousands for rent

Homelessness in Northern California
Has a whole new formula
Not just low-income folks
The middle-class workers
Have nowhere to hang their coats

The middle-class workers
Have nowhere to hang their coats

GAIL WASSERMAN

Burning the Midnight Oil

Heard the alarm clock ring
That annoying ding ding ding
Saw the moon shining bright
Reminding me to work tonight

Burning the midnight oil
So our dreams won't be spoiled
This is what I have to do
To give my wife and kids
That quality kind of life

Sitting at the computer desk
With no time to rest
Banging on the keys
To make the extra money

Burning the midnight oil
So our dreams won't be spoiled
This is what I have to do
To give my wife and kids
That quality kind of life

Never thought a guy like me
Would care about family

Burning the midnight oil
So our dreams won't be spoiled
This is what I have to do
To give my wife and kids
That quality kind of life

Gail Wasserman is a poet/ lyricist from California. Gail serves on the Board of Benicia Literary Arts and has several publications in the Benicia Herald, Moonstone Arts Center, Read and Green Books Press, the Chelsea Underground and numerous other anthologies. In addition, Gail received Honorable Mention in the Ina Coolbrith 2022 and 2023 Poetry Contests.

PANIC IN THE YEAR ZERO

a 1960s movie soon the sci fi dust bowl
"Grapes of Wrath" with burner phones
& wifi hot spots
families in SVUs
pitched tents on freeway slopes
blue tarps of despair
Thom's neighbor can't cut hair
so now $40 blow jobs
but my neighbor
no mask, no social distance
showing off his cherry
50s Plymouth
like a talisman

Marc Olmsted has appeared in *City Lights Journal, New Directions in Prose & Poetry, New York Quarterly, The Outlaw Bible of American Poetry and* a variety of small presses. He is the author of six collections of poetry, including *What Use Am I a Hungry Ghost?*, which has an introduction by Allen Ginsberg. Olmsted's 25 year relationship with Ginsberg is chronicled in his Beatdom Books memoir *Don't Hesitate: Knowing Allen Ginsberg 1972-1997 - Letters and Recollections*, available on Amazon.

DAILY WAGE WORKER

Bamboo stick arms with muscle strength
drag, heave, lift and fling heavy bags
of rubble from broken walls
bricks, tiles, pipes and more

Two men load truck, another sifts
tiles from bricks, pipes from hinges
finds a treasure – torn yoga mat
the only blue among greys
that would depress
me and you

He holds it up against the sun
wraps it around his waist for fun
carefully folds it in two and four
lays it on the rough truck floor
uses it as it should be used
a mat on which he sat.

Beside him lies a tattered cement bag
Filled with hinges, handles, wires, pipes
Scrap for one, is gold for others
a kilo of metal fetches the price
for three sparse meals tonight.

These daily wage workers are the spine of my country
Not magnets in glass-steel structures scraping skylines.
At roadsides, fields, construction sites,
They toil, struggle, strive for a decent life
While making homes for city-zens luxurious lives

Meher Pestonji has been a journalist, novelist, playwright, and short story writer. She weaves issues of contemporary relevance – street kids, communal harmony, war and peace – into her diverse forms of writing hoping to contribute to making our planet safer, more inclusive.

CITIZENS WHO LOOK LIKE ME

through african roots
from planted seed
i bloomed from youth
into learning tree
but across the waters
of middle passage route
under caribbean waves
where i seek the truth
i can't find my way
can't pull up my boots
by straps the ancestors left
that were supposed to support
but are thin, slippery and wet
i'm feeling lost and forsaken
like waiting for the next plane
while sitting in the subway station
like when i can't find my place
in this cold water nation
they freeze me out
when i try integration
and if huddle with others for
the warmth of equality
there's only limited inclusivity
for too many citizens
who look like me
so i wonder
can i always be my best
when some with flesh
of a much lighter degree
continue to block
the rest of citizens
who look like me
of basic needs that lead to liberty?
battles won in the 1960's
get lost as years succeed
civil rights now whittled
down to little figurines
because many of us find it hard
these days to afford
the high cost of being free
which always seems
out of reach and ever-fleeting
for too many citizens
who look like me

REMOTE CONTROL

if we remain compliant and silent
and allow those with evil eyes
to feed us mayhem and violence
while we watch the world slip by
one foot on a banana peel
one eye on the channel guide
while we're busy binge-watching
netfix, hulu and amazon prime
or some other premium service
to which we've recently subscribed
will we be paying enough attention
so we don't get fooled next time
when ol' jim crow re-appears
dressed to kill, pressed to the 9s
trying to impress like
he's this phi-beta alum from
some bogus college online
who re-invented himself as
the new james crow, esquire,
sporting 3-piece suit, bow tie
with false teeth, dyed hair,
empty promises and fake smile
trying his best to keep us convinced
he's cared about our welfare all the while
unless we happen to be on welfare
then we're stepped to the rear of the line
next to the door marked "marginalized"
too many fail to realize
that while we're ever ready
to be stars on reality tv
we're not so ready for prime time
we remain dumb, thinking we can switch
between live and rerun
and not be undermined
or sold some bill of goods
that ain't no damn good
will never turn gold
or be worth anything more
than a block of salt brine
we can only move past status quo
once we stop pressing rewind
and letting an old remote do its best
to keep us controlled, mentally stressed
buying more, getting less
programmed for another
soap opera drama

as the world turns
a dumb tongue, deaf
ear and blind eye
continuing to deny our rights
in hopes we die right before
we get to collect our social security prize

but meantime,
don't forget to set your dvr
i heard tonight at 9
the revolution will be televised
and you can see it live
but only if you subscribe
to starz

Gregory Pond was born in Brooklyn to Panamanian parents, has written five books of poetry and is a member of Revolutionary Poets Brigade. He hosts *3rd Saturday Poetry in Chinatown,* facilitates *Poetically Speaking* - a weekly conference-call program for seniors, and has curated events for Queer Rebels. He currently resides in San Francisco.

Rosso

Del rosso abbondante in strade morenti
del rosso di cuori che non vedono sole
del rosso di sole che non vedono cuori
di cuori al macello
di albe infuocate da spari di cielo
di rosso del sangue di fuochi
di giochi
di rosso del sangue d'una vita
che nasce
di rosso della madre che muore
di rosso annerito da miniere e sudori
del rosso del vino che ha sconfitto
la vita
del rosso del vino che ubriaco di te
del rosso di palco di sera da sballo
di rosso d'amore a volte al tuo fianco
del rosso tramonto che scambia
i miei giorni
del giorno che vita che mi riporta a te
del rosso di luce di quadri d'autore
di rosso di fiamma al camino che scalda
del rosso di croce quand'è solidale
di rosso che brucia ma non porta calore
di rosso d'un fiore per errore raccolto
di rosso di viscere di lava
alla terra che lava
di rosso chiarore che esplodendo non vedi
di rosso che vesti quando svesti il pudore
di rosso di labbra che apri alle labbra
del rosso ferita al tuo ventre e così
la mia vita comincia

RED

Red abundant in dying streets
red of hearts that don't see the sun
red of sun that don't see hearts
of hearts at the slaughter
of fiery dawns of shots in the sky
red the blood of a life
that is born
red of a mother who dies
blackened red of mines and sweat
red of wine drunk of you
red of nightly dance stage
red of love sometimes at your side
red the sunset that exchanges
my days
with the day of life that takes me back to you
red of light of authors' paintings
red of flames in the chimney that warms up the air
red of a cross when it's sympathetic
red that burns but doesn't bring heat
red of a flower picked by mistake
red of innards of lava
on the earth that it washes
red the dim light that exploding you don't see
red you wear when you undress modesty
red of lips that you open to the lips
red the wound in your womb and in this way
my life begins.

Beppe Costa was born in Sicily and lives in Rome. In 1976 he founded the publishing house Pellicanolibri and in 1992 he opened its relevant bookshop. As a publisher, he published works by notorious poets, journalists and writers such as Fernando Arrabal, Manuel Vàsquez Montalbàn, Gaston Bachelard, Gisele Halimi, Naim Araidi. But also Alberto Moravia, Dario Bellezza, Arnoldo Foà, Adele Cambria, Anna Maria Ortese, Goliarda Sapienza.  Beppe Costa's poetry collections and short stories have been published extensively.

Beppe Costa è nato in Sicilia e vive a Roma. Nel 1976 fonda la casa editrice Pellicanolibri e nel 1992 ne apre la relativa libreria. Come editore, ha pubblicato opere di noti poeti, giornalisti e scrittori come Fernando Arrabal, Manuel Vàsquez Montalbàn, Gaston Bachelard, Gisele Halimi, Naim Araidi. Ma anche Alberto Moravia, Dario Bellezza, Arnoldo Foà, Adele Cambria, Anna Maria Ortese, Goliarda Sapienza. Le raccolte di poesie e i racconti di Beppe Costa sono stati ampiamente pubblicati.

Psalm to a Nonviolent Revolution

To Jack Hirschman and his son David

They hate workers
They despise unions
They paid off the Supreme Court
And the president of the United States
is in their back pockets
like so many cheap cigars.
They are the oligarchs
and they want to rule the world!
One of the oligarchs
is worth more than 300 billion dollars.
At the inauguration he gave the president
the Nazi salute in front of millions of people
And he had a big smile on his face
while the president grinned as his lips said
"Welcome to the new Republican Party... The party of Lincoln."

The working class,
that grizzly bear, is asleep
hibernating in a warm cave
waiting for cherry blossom spring
while some of the *pie cards* are trying
to sell out the working class,
as are the born-again Christians
and the fascist cops with their billy clubs and automatic rifles.

Yet the working class
will come out of hibernation
and the oligarchs *will tremble.*
Only the hidden eye
in the middle of the forehead
can see the future
and know if the working class and its allies
can finally throw off their chains
and tear down everything
that must be destroyed.
And it will happen when the oligarchs
are nothing but *demonic lies!*

David Volpendesta is a nonviolent anarchist who carries a bazooka with his pen! He is a member of the Revolutionary Poets Brigade and has been included in all the anthologies. His publications include Astralphonic Voices, Dawn in the Night, Volcan, and Forbidden Psalms.

BUILT

An open letter to the education systems in the states of Texas & Florida

Riddle me this:

WHICH IS WORSE?

Being depicted in
    History lessons
        As villains

OR

Being erased from
    History lessons
        Completely?

WHICH?

Your grade schools
    Are veering
        In that direction.

It's the 2nd stage following
    The gradual erasing
        Of Blacks from reality –

By cop,
    By bigot,
        By our own hands,

WE ARE BEING ERASED.

    Now we're not
        Allowed to keep records
            Or teach our young on them!

NOT IN YOUR CLASSROOMS.

By statewide,
    Countywide bans,
        By firing teachers who dare to share,

OUR HISTORY IS STAYS BURIED.

    The grasp of truth
        About this land's beginnings
            Sacrificed

DEE ALLEN.

FOR YOUR CHILDREN'S COMFORT.

Lest we forget,

By force AND
Force of will,
My people constructed

This country's, this state's,
This city's, this town's
Infrastructure

Your people,
Prejudiced people,
Claim as

YOUR GREAT ACHIEVEMENTS.

As sure as
Sunset brings
Day to an end,

My ancestors have built
All your blue eyes survey.

As sure as
Descendants of the
United Slaves to Amerikkka want reparations,

My ancestors have built
All your blue eyes survey.

BLACK HANDS

Have raised your sky-scraping
Buildings from the ground on up,
Paved your roadways w/ cement & gravel,
Pieced together those strong, sturdy
Iron bridges over water, the ones
You cross on morning & evening commutes,
Drove buses, trains & cable cars
To send YOU to work, home &
The neighborhood bar,
Toiled in your factories, warehouses,
Offices & power plants,
Rocked your loud, crying babies to sleep,

Cleaned from front to back
The rooms of YOURHOMES,
Laid down miles of iron track & wood,
Hammered in the spikes for
Railroads along w/ yellow hands
For the same criminally low wage,
Tended to open fields of vegetation –
Vegetables, grains, fruits, sugarcane
& yes, King Cotton –
So all of you can eat well
& wear decent clothes –

1 city in particular –
    Former home of mine –
        Was burnt to a crisp in

A war between states –
    Arose from war's ashes
        Like a phoenix in the southeast

ATLANTA

Rebuilt
    W/ work
        From Black prisoners, White corporate punishment -

SLAVERY SURVIVED IN ANOTHER FORM.

Conflict like this,
    Between races,
        Between classes,

Lie @ the heart
    Of Amerikkka's & Capitalism's
        Conjoined past –

As sure as
    Wet & dry
        Are opposite feelings,

My ancestors have built
    All your blue eyes survey.

Including your schools.

Riddle me this:

HOW LONG

Do you think
    Your laws can prevent
        Truth from reaching young ears?

HOW LONG?

The spotlight
    Is
        Switched off

On tales of Europe,
    The original 13 colonies,
        The 1st Thanksgiving dinner.

EUROCENTRISM STOPS HERE.

One-sided
    Stars & stripes Liberty
        Sugarcoat from your schools

Sweetened young minds
    Enough to forget
        Their own struggle to survive here –

Riddle me this

1 last thing:

W/out our hands,
    W/out our legwork,
        W/out our labor,

HOW WILL YOUR CIVILIZATION RUN?

W: New Year's Eve 2022

Dee Allen. African-Italian performance poet based in Oakland, California. Active on creative writing & Spoken Word since the early 1990s. Author of 10 books--Boneyard, Unwritten Law, Stormwater, Skeletal Black, Elohi Unitsi, Rusty Gallows: Passages Against Hate, Plans, Crimson Stain, his most recent Discovery and coming in January 2025, The Mansion – and 77 anthology appearances under his figurative belt so far.

RISING VOICES

In shadows cast by hands unseen,
The workers toiled; hearts heavy, worn.
Chains of gold, their faces mean,
In silence, we are but scorned.

The workers toiled; hearts heavy, worn.
Our voices whisper in the dark.
In silence, we are but scorned.
Yet in our chests, a quiet spark.

Our voices whisper in the dark.
A storm brews in the quiet night.
Yet in our chests, a quiet spark,
We rise against oppressive might.

A storm brews in the quiet night,
Chains of gold, their faces mean.
We rise against oppressive might,
In shadows cast by hands unseen.

CHRISTINE MARIE MAGPILE

ROAR OF SOLIDARITY

In the shadows, we toil, we labor.
Our silent suffering, bound in chains.
Whispers echo, a clash of sabers,
Hope ignites as freedom gains.

Our silent suffering, bound in chains.
A tremor, a rumble in our souls.
Hope ignites as freedom gains.
The unified cry of shared goals.

A tremor, a rumble in our souls,
Together we rise, we won't fall.
The unified cry of shared goals,
Through unity, we break the wall.

Together we rise, we won't fall,
Whispers echo, a clash of sabers.
Through unity, we break the wall,
In the shadows, we toil, we labor.

Christine Marie Lim Magpile is a teacher, book editor-author, translator, and creative writer. She has a BS Education – History (cum laude) from the University of Santo Tomas, Manila. She has completed her academic requirements for MA in Counseling at De La Salle University. Presently she is preparing her thesis proposal for her MA in Araling Pilipino from the University of the Philippines, Diliman. She is a fellow of several national writers' workshops in the Philippines such as the Iligan National Writers Workshop (2024), DLSU Young Screenwriters Workshop (2023), La Salle Kritika National Workshop on Art and Cultural Criticism (2019), 6th Angono Writers' Summer Workshop (2018), the UST National Writers' 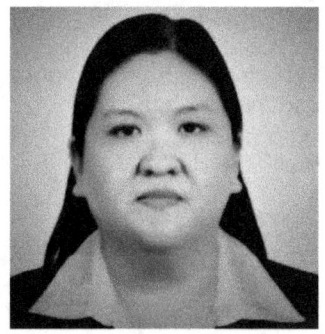 Workshop (2008), and the Linangan, Imahe, Retorika, at Anyo (LIRA, 2007 and 2023). Magpile won third place at the 2022 Sanaysay ng Taon from the Komisyon sa Wikang Filipino (KWF). She was a finalist for the Salita ng Taon in 2010 (load), 2014 (kalakal), and 2016 (foundling). She was a finalist for the 2013 Readers Choice Awards for her children's fiction, *Kayumanggi*. Presently, Magpile is a University Researcher III and editor from UP Diliman and project-based language editor and proofreader from the UP Sentro ng Wika-Diliman.

Betty's Fed Up

Betty's fed up with the way her boss talks to her,
the way this liver spot of a customer is consistently rude to her,
Betty has had enough this afternoon; Betty brought some kerosene
in her lunch thermos. Smoke is gray and billowing everywhere.
Look: register number six is now on fire. *So pretty.*
The customer must suck it up and go crawl somewhere else today.
Betty's fed up, see? The star-shaped scale at register six
is melting. No one quite knows what to do.
The manager's trying to find Betty but he's lost the game.
Betty's actually behind the wheel of her car right now
and she's driving home. Driving home unencumbered and free.
You don't have to deal with rude and threatening customers
if the register is on fire and the store is filling up with the smell
of burning metal, melting plastic and asshole customers denied.
This is the story about a legend who got pushed too far.
This is the story about a boss who learned the hard way
to shut his God-damned mouth and do better.
This is the story of a man who didn't deserve to live
because he loved being a rude customer
and he's not with us anymore.
There are so many things to learn from this story.

Betty was fed up.

Betty took control of a red situation
and made it baby blue.

Be like Betty.

Rich Boucher

VENGEANCE IS OURS

When the customers come
with their Gold Card cruelty
and their rubberlipped rudeness,
when they come to your register
sauntering self-satisfied and wearing their condescension
at a jaunty angle on the top of their heads
with their vicious lies and pompous mouths,
when they brandish their teeth and snarl at you
when they come to snap their fingers at you
like all you are is another dog they own
because they know
in the mildewed basements of their hearts
that they can demand that your manager
order you to suck on them and smell their boots
be steady, be upright and strong for as long as you can
because the time is coming:
it won't be too much longer;
the calendar can only hold so much misery
and you will know that the day is getting near,
understand and hear,
look for the waxing half-moon in the late evening sky
wearing a mask of blood and garnet and amber,
by this you'll know that the day without light
will be the next day and it will come even if the Sun does not
so be ready, be ready to join the fight
when the Houses of Retail and Customer service
align cosmically inside the Second House
and the Second House's windows explode outward –
cover your nose and mouth with a rag,
it's time to serve some special cocktails,
better realize that the war isn't coming; it's already *here,*
be ready with a bat or a chain or a whip
for the day of grey clouds, cold winds,
it's prophesied that the Karens and Darrens of this world
are going to get their teeth kicked in at last,
be ready for the sign
the time is so close, almost upon us,
buy a mannequin or dummy
to keep at home,
practice whipping someone in the face
think about the customer
when you practice whipping across a back
remember every time one of them
threatened you
or mocked you because of your *nametag life*
be ready to *get some*

be ready to *take some*

a century from now
they'll study in freshly printed,
mimeograph-smell textbooks
how we made the customers
weep and wail
and bleed and kneel

how we made them surrender
how we made them disappear

 **Rich Boucher** resides in Albuquerque, New Mexico. Rich's
poems have appeared in The Nervous Breakdown, Eighteen
Seventy, Menacing Hedge, The Rye Whiskey Review and
Cultural Weekly, among others, and he has work
forthcoming in Pulp Literary Magazine and Eunoia Review.
Rich recently served as Associate Editor for the online
literary magazine BOMBFIRE. He is the author of All Of
This Candy Belongs To Me, a collection of poems published
by Jules' Poetry Playhouse Publications.

Peep richboucher.bandcamp.com for more. He loves his life
with his love Leann in the perpetually intriguing Southwest.

CATCHING A RIDE TO WORK

He stood on the corner by the posh department store
Clutching his brown-bagged lunch.
Behind him stood the mannequins
Dressed in their cold stares and upper class sophistication.
He felt their plaster pulses, pushing him away
As though they didn't deem him worthy to
Wait before their exclusivity.
"Go across to the Five and Dime," they taunted.

Their fake smiles froze, as Wind's snowy bits of artistry
Sought shelter 'neath his blue-collared existence.
It seemed these flawless flakes felt no shame
In touching his belabored skin.

He held the road with his eyes
Hoping its macadam mirage would insulate him
From the glare of these stagnant accusers
Who modeled their self-righteousness for the worthy.

He thought of his kids who forced his tired form
Out into the 6:00A.M. cold.
He fought the urge to melt into the cold concrete
That jeered up at him. "Come on. Lie down. They'll never miss you."

Then two lights blazed the flurried darkness
And to an ageless audience
The man auditioned with a smile. (An old routine yet well performed.)
He'd gladly leave the stage to actors more refined.

The sole chauffeur he'd ever known
Spoke in rave reviews.
"Hi, Joe! Sorry I'm late."
"That's OK," the old boy lied. He felt the factory calling.
Perhaps today, they'd zoom right past
That mechanized enslavement of his spirit.
With one last glance at the ladies in lace,
He knew that he, too, was in costume.
"Pay day, Joe!" the young voice nudged
Drags on his smoke foul the air.
"Yea," Joe sighed, eyes tearing on second-hand sorrow.
"I'm gonna win the big one, ya know," his rider chided.
"Well, I hate to disappoint you
But I've got the lucky ticket right here,"
Joe teased, as he pledged his shirt pocket.
They laughed right along with the worn out Chevy.

"The big fight's tonight.
You ain't gonna miss it?"
"I ain't missed one yet," Joe replied.
"I got me a front row seat."
"Yea? Me too!" Joe laughed. "An ice cold beer's just wait'n."
The rider grinned. "I can almost taste it."
Funny, how their hollow rhetoric soothed with its mediocrity.

Joe's large, calloused hand found the brown, pocketed beads.
(The ones he'd had since first communion, many years ago.)
He sighed submissively to their sweet surrogate touch.
"You're not alone, Joe. You're not alone," they chanted.

He felt a twinge of pity for all the mannequins
Who reigned o're all the vacuumed vanities of the world,
For, neither would they know
The Friday-night flights of the arm-chaired welterweight,
Nor the Love that kept him rising from that chair.

FEEDING THE PIGEONS

He looked to the sky with his questions,
Released them like doves at a wake.
He looked to the pundits who toyed with the news, but
Their mortar rounds skewed the debate.

He looked to the campus for knowledge,
Mortgaged his life to the muse.
He looked to the sea for recovery and rest
Yet she pushed him right back toward the dunes.

He looked to his parents for guidance
To go where they never had been.
He looked to his kids for incentives
To do what meant nothing to them.

He looked to the forests that rushed past his view
Thinking, "Someday, those woods'll be mine."
Yet, someday, those woods might not even be there
And in fear he felt so rushed for time.

He looked to the birds for distraction
From worries he just didn't need.
He looked to the park bench to slow the world down
And a bag lady gave him some seed.

"Thank you," he said, trying not to sound trite
As he scattered seeds 'round like a child.
And then, "What a great day!" and he meant every word!
"You better believe it," she smiled.

"You live around here?" he asked awkwardly.
Her smile had revealed missing teeth.
"Yep. I got me a place 'ere on Second Street South.
The dang pipes froze up 'oh last week.

I come here to get me away from the crowds.
'Course, I ain't complainin' none though.
Why, I gets me a good meal least once't ever' week
And these pigeons here need me. Ya' know?"

"Hi, Polly!" another came greeting. They hugged,
And with chirping for music, they danced.
Why, the old "soft shoe" stage never had it so good.
The man watched in wonder, entranced.

"How could they possibly know how to laugh,
With all of their pain and rejection?
Yet, maybe it's laughter that acclimates love
And maybe it's love that protects them."

He gave her his scarf and some money to spend,
And somehow he felt much less hurried.
See, he'd met the "Queen of the Park" on that day.
He'd forgotten just why he'd been worried.

She was part of the earth, while he'd merely used it.
Sure. She lacked the Park Avenue grammar.
Yet, he envied the pigeons their caretaker friend,
Who'd adorned Central Park with such glamour.

 **Jody Walker** is a retired elementary school teacher who was born and raised in Frostburg, MD. She has felt drawn to writing from a very early age not realizing that it was a tool that allows one to enter into deeper dimensions. She has always loved the "questions" and through art as contemplative practice she has learned to be open to solitude. "Writing," she says, "requires patience. It's an intentional retreat in which I am slowly learning to trust myself." Walker lives in Cumberland with her husband, Carey. They have two wonderful children, Amy Wilkinson and Brad Walker and two grands, Evan and Kendall. She's the author of Sophie, Milo and the Great Change and The Book of Mem.

DEAR AMERICA,

So you want a fascist state?
So you want a strong man?
So you want a daddy?
So you want a leader?
Why don't you lead yourself?
Why don't you follow your heart not hatred?
Where is the independent American spirit?
Where is the rugged individualism?

It's out there on the open road, the open mind,
the free spirit that sees it's country for itself not letting
the screen tell it what to feel, think, and say.

Don't let the Constitution be for nothing.
Don't let Due Process be for nothing.
Don't let Civil Rights be for nothing.
Don't let Roe vs. Wade be for nothing.
After our grandfathers in WW2 saved the world from fascism,
will you really let this country become a fascist state?
In a nation of immigrants will you really stand by as our
Latino brothers and sisters are detailed without trial?
Don't let workers' rights won be for nothing.
Don't let freeing the slaves be for nothing.
Don't let the American Revolution be for nothing.

Casting off shackles, casting out kings, the
American Revolution is still happening!
There is so much more to do.
There is so much more to liberate.
And if you let this country slip into
an authoritarian state...
We, the free thinkers
will take it back.

Westley Heine is the author of *Busking Blues: Recollections of a Chicago Street Musician and Squatter* (Roadside Press 2022), and a short story collection *12 Chicago Cabbies* (Newington Blue Press 2021). Most recently Roadside Press has released a poetry collection *Street Corner Spirits* (2023), and a new collection of short stories and poems entitled *Cloud Watching in the Inferno* (2025), both of which have spoken word albums available on all streaming services.

Nothing Great About Depression

From a distance she was small with her hand raised high
we could hear her calling and speaking in tongues
"brothers and sisters, we are ALL ONE"
remove an L – we are ALONE
the delicate state of camaraderie
we changed our names at the pearly gate
and thanked our god for bringing us home

We've been digging holes ever since that day
covered with dirt as it piled up around us
somebody made money off of our grunts and hollers
we never complained and we survived

We were soldiers in the mines way down south
some lost their fingers some lost an eye
but we held tightly to the reason why
the little ones playing in the yard
soon enough the time would be right
for the predators waiting to take a bite

Come here not to preach an obscene homily
or to justify the unjust suffering
from the strawberry fields in California
to the black lung disease of West Virginia
they lived half their life in a cold black cave
I know what it means to be 'underground'

What is the life expectancy
in the factories of industry
a construction worker, a farm laborer
a homeless beggar on the city sidewalk
a sweating child in a ghetto shop

At the age of 20 I joined the Teamsters
we moved iron rods from one building to another
all day long from one building to another
all year long from one building to another
we were a Team, it took 6 men to carry one iron bar
we lifted high and walked together, nobody slacked
we were carrying our cross to Semana Santa
we were in the union, we were unified, in solidarity
nothing could stop us, we were building bridges
singing "I'd Love to Change the World" with Alvin Lee

When creatures work together, they move mountains
in Appalachia they move mountains

in The Republic of China, they move mountains
on the African continent they move mountains
in the Arabian desert mountains are moved
in South American rain forests they move mountains
the truth remains that you cannot stop creatures
from moving mountains, they exist to be moved

Solidarity requires resistance and rebellion
defiance, the opposite of repression
solidarity must be a defense
solidarity must be defended
this responsibility lies in every movement
every shovel filled with soil
every pot of soup that boils
every child that gazes at the stars
every book of poetry on every carpenter's shelf

Freedom demands solidarity
the courage to trust the outreached hand
to fill the street with righteous protest
to fill the street with music and dance
a written history in the halls of justice

There shall be no dictation received from any source
no cruelty against the spoken word
no obstacle set before common progress
the threat of pain or power of fear
shall not overcome a brave new heart

Let nature be the clear example
let nature tell its glorious tale
let us huddle together on the frozen plain
let us link our arms across the canyon
let us form an army of unstoppable force

Knowledge and wisdom, our currency
shall be our fortune in urgency
collectively constructing a living platform
free of all discrimination
from Harlem to Harlan let us raise our flag
philia, agape, a renaissance
the philosopher stood and testified
that death was preferred to a life of lies
and worse than death to live in vain
forsaking the citizens bound in chains
we shall live this life in noble service
and thus denounce the oppressor's gain

We are not here to speak in vulgar tongues
or parrot the tired phrases of men
excitement, tragedy, glory, and horror
the energy of hate better spent in deployment
the fallen angels of revolution be honored

So, in our calm and peaceful moment
we clothe our frames in the light of love
lift our tools and our pens as weapons
our voices ringing our testimonial
that we shall never surrender, never rest
and in our numbers, we find the strength
to march into the battle that never ends
now as one, we sign this manifest

Joe Kidd is a working poet / songwriter / artist. He's been awarded by the Michigan Governor's Office and the United States House of Representatives for his efforts to promote social justice, cultural diversity, and world peace. Joe was appointed Beat Poet Laureate State of Michigan 2022-2024. He has been named Official Poet and Ambassador of Peace by the Government of Birland North Africa. Joe holds Honorary Doctorate from International Peace Federation and Writer's Union. He is ordained in a non-denominational church. Joe Kidd has received numerous awards including: Songwriter of the Year, 2024 Platinum Eagle Award, Champion of Diversity Award from Images & Perceptions Organization. He is a Pushcart Prize nominee  2025. He has toured 9 countries in Western Europe. Also Canada, Mexico and 33 states in America, as well as Jamaica. He has been featured in international anthologies, magazines, websites, festivals, and other personal appearances worldwide. Joe is a member of National & International Beat Poetry Foundation, 100 Thousand Poets For Change, Society of Classical Poets, International Singer Songwriter Association, Michigan Rock & Roll Hall Of Fame. Joe Kidd has published 2 full length books. In 2020, published The Invisible Waterhole, a collection of spiritual and sensual verse. In 2024, published a short auto biography titled 'Digging Underground – Portrait of a Beat Poet Laureate'.

I Bet You They'd Try

you can't squeeze
blood from a
turnip,
but i bet you
they'd try;

billionaires don't want
to pay their fair share
in taxes
but they're willing to take
what little we have to make
themselves richer –

is it really such a mystery
to them why we hate them?

i'll never kiss the boots
of the person who
kicked me,

that's for sure;

all my life i have been working
since i was sixteen and i paid into
my retirement plan and social security
and i deserve to have both when
i'm older –

billionaires paying their taxes would
still have billions,
it's about time these people pay
their fair share.

Linda M. Crate

Against All Odds

people trying to say
i have to feel bad
for the ceo and his family,

why?

do you think they gave
one crap when they denied
people life-saving health care?

no, they probably celebrated
another claim getting denied;

the person they killed was
someone else's entire
world –

so, no, i won't ever cry over
any billionaires death;

the people whose names
we should remember are the
common every day people like
me and you –

the people who fight to
make the world a better place
against all odds.

Linda M. Crate (she/her) is a Pennsylvanian writer whose poetry, short stories, articles, and reviews have been published in a myriad of magazines both online and in print. She has twelve published chapbooks the latest being: Searching Stained Glass Windows For An Answer (Alien Buddha Publishing, December 2022).

L'ERA DEL GLICINE

Contemplando gli dèi solidi delle città notturne
e il cranio giallo sopra le dinamo incendiarie
dei lampioni, nello spettro riarso delle strade,
nel grigio delle tarde ore rastrellano i cantonieri
con la forza muta di un Patroclo, nell'arsura
del grande cosmo, sotto una spenta luna
con sugli zigomi il duro sudore dell'asfalto!,
dove gemono al vento, come serrate in fila,
piantate tamerici. Attorno sbarre di lamiere,
poi lingue di carreggiate, ospedali fabbriche
di nuovo fabbriche, lingue di carreggiate
serpi di rotatorie come intestini urbani
e ancora lo stomaco ferroso d'altre fabbriche,

le unghie dormienti dei prefabbricati
dove riposano le vite nei cimiteri dimenticati,
membra che hanno stretto sulle labbra
i loro sigari di piombo fumante, in faccia
a questa volta celeste, tra artificiali nembi.
Una città riposa, quella delle bollette
e delle motrici in coda. Una città salpa
con la sua viscida prua di bettola
e le tasche rigonfie di sonno dei netturbini.
Riprende il sole a salire coi suoi tacchi d'oro
sopra le mura dei cieli, nel primo crepuscolo
di un giorno penetrante. Ronzano come rugginosi
calabroni gli autobus! Nell'urto feroce dei lavori
azzanna la fame delle ossa il grido dei disperati!

Con forza nuda, con rapace forza
lentamente si è spenta anche l'ultima primavera.
Non tornerà, se non con passo diverso, inudibile
nei fiori di quella che si appresta a venire.
Non sanno che dietro la semplice aurora
pedala un fornaio assonnato, sulla ruota dei raggi
nell'ora in cui nasce la fatica del pane.
Tace in quell'ora il mondo. Nel sonno delle notti
avviene l'impasto. Sino alla radice. Sino alla nuda
pietra dell'acqua. Leviga la corrente e scava,
penetra e permea, l'onda non cessa
attraverso la roccia, nella sua limpida forza.
Così, con lingua sporca di cieca materia
essi donano all'alba il loro giorno nascente,
l'inaudito siero della propria fragranza.
Alla pari l'eguagliano, mescolandosi, lettere e versi.

LORIS FERRI

Forgiate in assenza d'uomo, lontano dal rovente
ferro delle città, a grandi passi si popolano
le antiche foreste. Nel penetrante silenzio del buio
ululano i lupi alla luna e ringhiano ai temporali

THE AGE OF WISTERIA

Contemplating the solid gods of the nocturnal cities
and the yellow skull above the incendiary dynamos
of the streetlamps, in the parched spectrum of the streets,
the roadworkers are combing in the grey of the late hours
with the mute strength of a Patroclus, in the heat
of the great cosmos, under a dull moon
with hard sweat of asphalt on the cheekbones!,
where planted tamarisks groan in the wind,
as if closed in line. Around, bars of sheet metal,
then tongues of carriageways, hospitals, factories,
again factories, tongues of carriageways
serpents of roundabouts like urban intestines
and again the iron stomach of other factories,

the sleeping fingernails of the prefabs
where lives rest in forgotten cemeteries,
limbs that have tightened in the lips
their cigars of smoking lead, in the face
of this celestial sphere, between artificial clouds.
A city reposes, that of the bills
and of the engines in a queue. A city sets
with its slimy tavern prow
and the sleep-filled pockets of the street cleaners.
The sun recommences rising with its golden heels
above the walls of the skies, in the first dusk
of a penetrating day. The buses buzz
like rusty hornets! In the fierce clash of works
the hunger of bones bites down on the cry of the desperate!

With naked force, with rapacious force
slowly even the last spring is extinguished.
It won't return, if not with a different step, inaudible
in the flowers of that which is about to come.
They don't know that behind the simple dawn
pedals a sleepy baker, on the spoked wheel
at the hour when the toil of the bread is born.
It is silent in the world at that hour. In the sleep of the nights
the mixing takes place. Down to the root. Down to the bare
rock of the water. The current smooths and excavates,
penetrates and permeates, the wave doesn't cease
through the rock, in its limpid force.
Like this, with tongue dirty with blind matter
they give to the sunrise their nascent day,
the unheard serum of its own fragrance.
They equalize it, mixing, letters and verses.

Forged in the absence of man, far from the red hot
iron of the cities, in great steps it populates
the ancient forests. In the penetrating silence of the dark
the wolves howl to the moon and growl at the storms.

Loris Ferri was one of the editors of the literary
magazines << la Gru >> taking part in the project
Trampling on oblivion. He has published the books:
Borderline, Thauma 2008, with a preface by Gianni
D'Elia; *Correspondences on the margins of the West*,
Effigie 2011, dialogic poems with Stefano Sanchini,
with a Note by Roberto Roversi; *Rom: man*,
Sigismundus 2012; *Poem of the residence*,
Sigismundus 2016; *Cinema Sarajevo*, Ensemble
2022; *At the end of time*, NFC 2024 (a project for the
Italian Capital of the Culture). Currently he
collaborates with the international magazine of
migration << El Ghibli >>. He has taken the play
Song of the marginalised to theatres together with

Frida Neri and Massimo Zamboni. His poems appear in magazines and
anthologies, including *The Arcane Charm of Betrayed Love*, a tribute to Dario
Bellezza, Perrone 2006; *Italian Poets Underground*, Il Saggiatore 2006; *Poetry
against the blockade*, more than 100 cuban, italian and venezuelan voices, ebook
Argo libri 2020. In 2012 he was invited to the International Festival of Seville and
Mexico *Chilango Andaluz*. In 2017-2018 was selected for the Europen project
called: *Refest*, Images and Words on Refugee Routes. In 2019-2020 he was artistic
director of the *Sponde* International Festival. He has won the following prizes:
Marazza giovani 2013; Sédar Senghor 2017.

Loris Ferri ha fatto parte della redazione della rivista << La Gru >> prendendo
parte al progetto *Calpestare l'oblio*. Ha pubblicato i libri: Borderlinea, Thauma
2008, con una prefazione di Gianni D'Elia; *Corrispondenze ai margini
dell'Occidente*, Effige 2011, poema dialogico con Stefano Sanchini e una Nota di
Roberto Roversi; *Rom: uomo*, Sigismundus 2012; *Poema della residenza*,
Sigismundus 2016; Cinema Sarajevo, Ensemble 2022; *Alla fine del tempo*, NFC
2024 (progetto realizzato per la Capitale Italiana della Cultura). Attualmente
collabora con la rivista internazionale della migrazione << El Ghibli >>. Ha preso
parte al progetto teatrale *Canto degli emarginati* con Frida Neri e Massimo
Zamboni. Le sue poesie sono apparse su riviste e antologie, tra cui *L'arcano
fascino dell'amore tradito*, omaggio a Dario Bellezza, Perrone 2006; *Poeti Italiani
Underground*, Il Saggiatore 2006; *Poesia contro il blocco*, più di cento voci
cubane, italiane, venezuelane, Argo ebook 2020. Nel 2012 è stato invitato al
Festival Internazionale di Siviglia e Messico *CHilango Andaluz*. Nel 2017-2018 è
stato scelto per il Progetto Europeo *Refest*, Parole e Immagini sulle Rotte dei
Rifugiati. Nel 2019-2020 è stato direttore artistico del Festival Internazionale
Sponde. Ha vinto i premi: Marazza giovani 2013; Sédar Senghor 2017.

INDUSTRY OF WAR

In the short time
Of preparing a meal,
Someone's home
Is being blown to bits.
I set the table
Light the candles
Taste a bite, savor potatoes,
Somewhere, there is weeping and gnashing of teeth.
I fill the goblet, lift the toast,
Recite the blessing,
While people are screaming, running, thirsting,
Salvaging body parts for holy rituals.
The money machine presses on
Souls the cost, no victory won
In solidarity, we pledge allegiance,
Continue working, paying taxes.
Turn off the news,
It's too unpleasant.
We're having a dinner
I can never digest.

SHEILA BURKE

WORKING MOM

There was a time when I believed
Every one, every word.
My own diminished voice still heard
Naive, I seemed, and yet, I dreamed.
I worked so hard and sold my soul
Life and times out of control.
Birthdays missed, kids recitals
Long, long hours, paycheck vital
Parents aging, gone and passed
Sick days lost, paychecks cashed.
Groping, harassing, backtalk and sassing
Always the hidden, intense agenda
My back is bent, no litigation
Job in jeopardy, the working mom's station.
Learning, sorting, drifting, enduring
Restless heart experimenting
Eventually trusting my senses more
The sacrifice worth the cost.
My soul redeemed, is mine at last

Sheila Burke is a working poet / songwriter / artist. She has been awarded by the Michigan Governor's Office and the United States House of Representatives for her efforts to promote social justice, cultural diversity, and world peace. Sheila was appointed Beat Poet Laureate State of Michigan 2024-2026, She has been named Official Poet and Ambassador of Peace by the Government of Birland North Africa. Sheila holds Honorary Doctorate from International Peace Federation and Writer's Union. She is ordained in a non-denominational church. Sheila has been named as one of 50 Most Memorable Women of North America. She has received numerous awards including: Songwriter of the Year, 2024 Platinum Eagle Award, Champion of Diversity Award from Images & Perceptions Organization. She is a Pushcart Prize nominee 2025. She has toured 9 countries in Western Europe. Also Canada, Mexico and 33 states in America, as well as Jamaica. She has been featured in international anthologies, magazines, websites, festivals, and other personal appearances worldwide. Sheila is a member of National & International Beat Poetry Foundation, 100 Thousand Poets For Change, International Singer Songwriter Association, Michigan Rock & Roll Hall Of Fame. With Joe Kidd, Sheila Burke released their first album titled. Everybody Has A Purpose in 2015. They have also been featured in compilation albums titled Songs For Standing Rock, and Music For Japan. Since then, they have periodically released a number of recordings including their latest release in January 2025, titled Liberation!

Крутятся Втулки

Крутятся втулки, наматывают на себя
цеховое время, снующее силуэтами
в синих спецовках – их бы назвать
«темно-синие», да темнота выкачана
насосами, гудящими коллективной речью
Крутятся втулки – и можно не думать
о морозе, о том, как провальный декабрь длится
уже без малого двести лет, можно слушать лектора
Мельтешение слайдов вот-вот протрёт
стену насквозь, мельтешение слайдов
станет вот-вот новой стеной
Крутятся втулки, вращением забираясь
всё глубже в мысли, но вот оно, знание
Синий цвет появился в природе в результате
рэлеевского рассеяния: в этом месте лекции
рабочие переспрашивают «рылеевского?»

THE HUBS KEEP SPINNING

The hubs keep spinning, winding around themselves
the factory's time, darting like silhouettes
in blue overalls – though one might call them
"dark blue," the darkness itself has been drained,
siphoned away by pumps that hum
with the collective voice of the workers
The hubs keep spinning – it helps to forget
the frost, the way a botched December
has dragged on for nearly two hundred years now
You can listen to the lecturer instead
The flickering of slides seems ready to wear
a hole clear through the wall,
their flickering about to become
a new wall of its own
The hubs keep spinning, their rotation burrowing
deeper into thought – until at last, knowledge arrives
Blue color appeared in nature, the lecturer explains,
thanks to Rayleigh scattering
At this point, the workers interrupt to ask,
"Ryleev* scattering?"

* Ryleev refers to Kondraty Ryleev (1795–1826), a Russian poet, writer, and
revolutionary. He was one of the leaders of the Decembrist revolt of 1825, an
uprising against autocratic rule and serfdom in Imperial Russia. Ryleev was
executed for his role in the rebellion, and his name has since become associated
with dissent and the struggle for justice.

Кто Вблизи Рассматривал Колючую Проволоку

Кто вблизи рассматривал колючую проволоку,
каждую безжалостную звёздочку её, узнавал
в четырехконечном силуэте букву *Икс*
Можно надеяться, от всего мира убережёт
материализованная, опредмеченная в металле
неизвестность, окружившая периметр завода
по образу тюрем сибирских, дальневосточных
и прочих регионов необъятной родины
У этого мира вроде как нет прочих
слов, проясняющих – что значит быть рабочим
Новая колючая проволока блестит на солнце
Директор завода может быть спокоен за свою
иномарку, и всё правильно – чего не сделаешь
ради покоя, ради его ровного прилива,
шуршащего зарубежным курортом только для своих
Кто очередную смену отстоял так же,
как правду отстаивают, тот вряд ли проповедовал
уточнение неизвестного через плоть
раздираемую, саднящую прикосновением к границе

THOSE WHO LOOKED CLOSELY AT THE BARBED WIRE

Those who looked closely at the barbed wire,
each of its merciless little stars, would recognize
in the four-pointed silhouette the letter X
One might hope that the materialized,
objectified *unknown* in metal would guard
the perimeter of the factory,
reminiscent of Siberian and Far Eastern
prisons, and other regions of the vast homeland
This world, it seems, has no other
words to clarify what it means –
to be a worker
A new barbed wire gleams in the sunlight
The factory director can rest easy about his
foreign car, and rightly so – what wouldn't you do
for peace, for its steady flow,
rustling like an exclusive foreign resort for the chosen few?
Those who stood through yet another shift,
as one stand for the truth,
likely did not preach
the clarification of the *unknown* through flesh
torn and stinging from contact with the boundary

Aleksey Porvin, born in 1982, is a celebrated Russian poet whose works bridge cultural and linguistic boundaries. His poetry, translated into English, has appeared in esteemed publications such as *World Literature Today, Cyphers, Saint-Petersburg Review, Ryga Journal, SUSS, Words Without Borders, Fogged Clarity, The Straddler, Action Yes*, and many others, earning him recognition on the global literary stage. Porvin is the author of six critically acclaimed poetry collections in Russian: *Darkness is White* (Argo-Risk Press, 2009), *Poems* (New Literature Observer Press, 2011), *The Sun of the Ship's Detailed Rib* (INAPRESS, 2013), *The Poem of Addressing. The Poem of Defining* (MRP, 2017), *Our Joy Cecile* (Ivan Limbakh Press, 2023), and *Song of the Brothers* (New Literary Observer, 2024). His first collection translated into English, *Live By Fire* (Cold Hub Press, 2011), introduced his evocative voice to a wider audience. Aleksey Porvin's work has been recognized with numerous accolades, including the prestigious Russian Debut Prize (2012) and shortlisting for the Andrey Bely Prize in 2011, 2014, and 2024. Through his vivid imagery and profound meditations on human experience, Porvin continues to inspire readers worldwide.

THE TIME IS NOW

The power is in our hands to build
a new world from our shared humanity.
Abolish all the institutions that glorify hate
whether corporation or wrapped in faith.

Return the riches to the working class
upon whose back their wealth was made.
Strip power from the warmongers
whose profit is drenched in our blood.

There's enough resources to go around
if only we free the world from these clowns.
All the people will be housed and fed,
once these greedy bastards are dead.

D.L. Lang is an internationally published poet who appears in over 95 anthologies worldwide. She is a three time Woody Guthrie Poet, member of the Revolutionary Poets Brigade, the IWW, CPUSA, and former poet laureate of Vallejo, California. Find her at poetryebook.com

For The People Of The Sun, Moon And Stars

For The People of The Sun, Moon and Stars
(Y)our Spirit can't be detained in unmarked cars
Rubber bullets leave scars
But still we find a way
To Unite and free them from the prison bars
Where's the Love?
Where's the compassion?
In gestapo squads with no warrants
Breaking down doors and smashing
In windows of opportunity
Break up dividing families
These People are our community
The enemy ain't The Unity
But sing it loudly
Yeah this is more like a eulogy
For any semblance of lies
They passing off as a Truth to me
We crushing ICE
With the fire of our heart's purity
The way our Spirit
See us in others with soul surity
The flames of fury
They moving in a flurry
But what's the driver
The People Untied
Can never be divided surely
We see with clear and sound minds
Fearless large hearts we doing what we can
Yeah our Intelligence is sharp
Shaper then this spears tip
We crushing and we rip
Apart the things that they fire
At us and try to make us trip
On division we ain't listening
We hearing what be persisting
That's Love in Us
That's raising fists n'
Helping hands
As we stand amongst the glistening
Shattered glass of a predatory system
The shots missed 'em
We just keep coming instead
We Warriors of Love
And we running with the wind's breath

THE SUN STILL RISES OVER PALESTINE

No matter how many bombs that they drop from the sky
The Sun Still Rises Over Palestine!
No matter how much death pierces all our eyes
The Sun Still Rises Over Palestine!
No matter how many people we been watching die
The Sun Still Rises Over Palestine!
No matter what they try to do to you and I
We sending Love to our Relatives in Palestine!
No matter how many lie
How they conquer and divide
The Sun Still Rises Over Palestine!
They try to occupy the land
But can't occupy our minds
The Sun Still Rises Over Palestine!
No matter how many times we seen a falling high-rise
The Sun Still Rises Over Palestine!
And no one can stop The Light
How it fills up your eyes
The way The Sun shines –
     From a Palestine Sunrise!

The Sun Still Rises Over Palestine
The Sun Still Rises in the Sky
The Sun Still Rises Over Palestine
The Sun Still Rises and it Shines
The Sun Still Rises Over Palestine
The Sun Still Rises in the Sky
The Sun Still Rises Over Palestine
And it's The Light of The Sun that Shines
That helps us see through the eyes of The People –
     That's Moving and Alive!

The Sun Still Rises
The Sun Still Shines
The Sun Still Rises
And no one can stop The Light
How it fills up your eyes
The way The Sun shines –
     From a Palestine Sunrise!

Chris Devcich is a musician and Hip Hop artist, MC, DJ, producer, editor, filmmaker, helper, disrupter, good eater and even, a poet... Member of Akicita Heyoka – the Fool Soldiers, an ancient warrior society based on nonviolence, here to help the people. As a member of many musical projects including the Luminaries, Truth & Love, C&A, and The Farmlife Project, Chris has performed on stages around the world from Pennsylvania to Palestine, alongside some of the greats.

THE WORLD THAT JACK BUILT

This is the world that Jack built.

This is the treasure
that lay in the world that Jack built.

These are the corporations
that stole the treasure
that lay in the world that Jack built.

These are the CEOs
who lead the corporations
that stole the treasure
that lay in the world that Jack built.

These are the stockholders
who pay the CEOs
who lead the corporations
that stole the treasure
that lay in the world that Jack built.

These are the laws
that enable the stockholders
who pay the CEOs
who lead the corporations
that stole the treasure
that lay in the world that Jack built.

These are the politicians
who write the laws
that enable the stockholders
who pay the CEOs
who lead the corporations
that steal the treasure
that lay in the world that Jack built.

These are the families abused and forlorn,
who suffer from poverty unadorned,
while politicians, with lies well-sworn
write laws with loopholes drawn
to enable stockholders, very well-born,
to pay CEOs, stylishly shorn,
to lead corporations, guilt forsworn,
and steal all the treasure
that lays in the world that Jack built.

So This is How it Feels

Despite or because
in the larger picture
we are them and they are us.

In a time of
mass murder and genocide.

Back in the old days
of daily print newspapers,
if you didn't like the headlines,
you could always turn
to the comics.

Almost out of butter.
Where did I put my keys?
Home team lost or won.
Celebrities filed for divorce.
The advice columnists
are scandalized.
Coffee cup needs washing.
Bananas are turning brown.
Late fees in the account.
Nails need trimming.

Keep walking in circles.
Past the expiration date.
Mailbox stuffed with junk again.
The everyday abuses
all around us in slow motion
at all times.
We can't go on like this.
We need to change this.
Immediately.
No one else is going to do it.
I've got to do something.
We've got to do something.
But what? But how?

After every hopeless disaster,
the world somehow
finds a way
to start over again.

So this is how it feels
to go about daily life
in 21st century America.

John Curl is the author of twelve poetry collections, including Rainbow Weather: Poems for Environmental Healing (Vagabond, 2022) and Revolutionary Alchemy (Homeward, 2012). His translations of ancient Inca, Maya, and Aztec poets are collected in Ancient American Poets (Bilingual Press, 2005). He is the author of two novels: The Outlaws of Maroon and The Co-op Conspiracy; Memories of Drop City (a memoir of the 1960s); For All The People, a history of cooperation in America, (PM Press, 2009); and Indigenous Peoples Day, a documentary history of the new holiday that he co-founded. He is a member of the Revolutionary Poets Brigade of San Francisco and co-editor of their annual poetry anthologies. He represented the USA at the World Poetry Festival in Venezuela in 2010.

KNOWLEDGE AND POWER

If only we'd known, they said
when the inmates of Belson
were first seen
in their
deliberately
ill-fitting
striped pajamas
dying from starvation,
dying from torture
dying from cold,
dying from illness,
dying
dying
dying.

If only we'd known, they said
when the extermination camps
were discovered,
the gas chambers,
the slave labour camps
where inmates were
killed
by over-work,
killed
by malnutrition
killed
by disease.

Exterminated.

If only we had known, they said,
there would have been no appeasement,
no 'peace in our time' self-protection,
no treaties for self-preservation,
no deals done in self-defense.
With the knowledge
intervention would have happened
genocide been prevented

if only we'd known.

Well this time we knew.
This time
we knew from the beginning.
This time
we knew from before the beginning,

LYNN WHITE

from long before the beginning
about the intimidation,
the arbitrary arrests,
homes demolished,
the camps filled
with innocents
left to die
from starvation,
illness or cold
or killed by torture.

Citizens bombed to death.
Nothing left but rubble.
No one left in the rubble.

And so we acted

to send arms
the perpetrators.

Lynn White lives in north Wales. Her work is influenced by issues of social justice and events, places and people she has known or imagined. She is especially interested in exploring the boundaries of dream, fantasy and reality. She has been nominated for Pushcarts, Best of the Net and a Rhysling Award.

LIGHTBULB

Like a flickering lightbulb
I'm on and off.
In life, like an animal about to be sold.
The crowd mock my woes;
They look down on me when I hope.
So, I remain unheard, unseen, a fading blow.

Doubts are my companion,
While I yearn for something alien.
That which my passion release and they cease.
At times, my fingers graze it and it feels like a dream,
Tugging my heart strings; I'm sure it is my calling dears.
One final step as it calls for me, so my name I hear.
Almost there, but it is never near.
For their whispers dim the lasting light I see.

A bulb condemned to flicker,
Why must I die for a quarter nickel?
Only for the mighty to demean what is left of fragile light;
Let me speak!
They are the reason I'm never steady.
Yet I have enough me to flicker,
Someday to shine bright and linger.

Ourarhi Chaymae is a Moroccan writer, researcher, and educator with a deep passion for literature, ecology, and philosophy. She is currently pursuing a PhD, where her research intertwines literary analysis and philosophical thought. Beyond academia, she is a dedicated poet, weaving themes of nature, human experience, and existential reflection into her work. Her love for literature and writing has led her to publish three poems in the Journal of Moroccan Chronicles, showcasing her lyrical and introspective style. Whether through scholarly inquiry or poetic expression, she remains committed to the power of words to inspire, question, and connect.

BLEED OUT

Enough already
Death is business
Governments send the young to bleed out
So the rich barons can increase their bank accounts
And no amount of spilled guts on foreign lands
Can account for empty families
destroyed in the name of ego
That pretends it is for freedom
The freedom to ban books but not guns
Business, you see
They want to free you and me
From what, we do not know
But they tell you so
So it must be true
As you may lose another
Sister or brother
As their coffers expand
With blood on the land

I served
I know
The futility of war
There is no gender in war
Just wasted lives

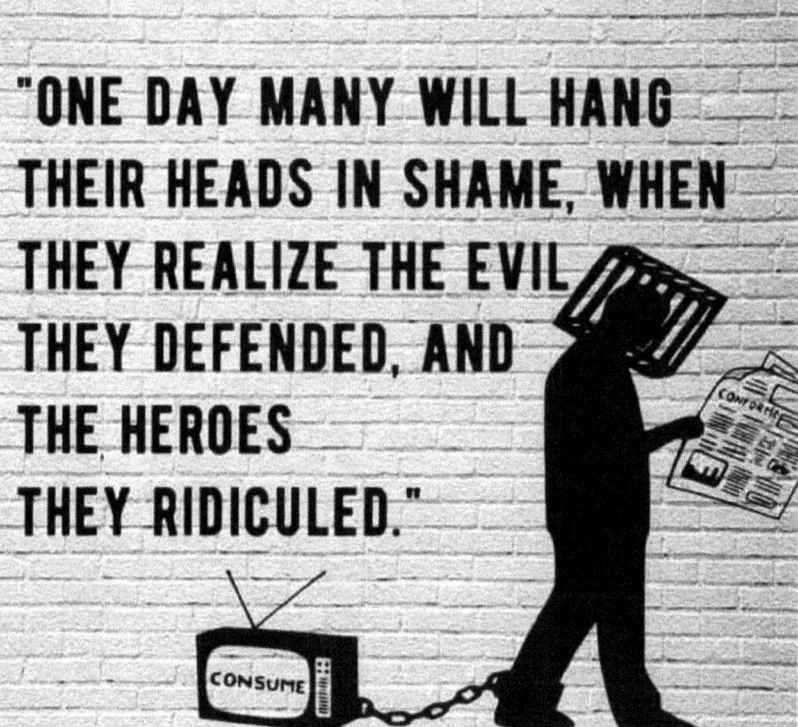

THIS

This and this and this and this, forever this.
Endless condescending comments
From those who have no concern for the suffering of others.
Excepting palms that bleed from so much praying
And heads that ache with all the thoughts
Forgetting that so many are descended from immigrants themselves
Who struggled and fought for a better life
That now they want to deny others.

Where those who weren't fortunate to be born with a gold,
or silver, or platinum, or even good quality stain less steel spoon
in their mouths
Must take what they are given
Not take what they need
Even those from professional backgrounds,
Doctors, Lawyers et al
Who's skills are not respected in their country of arrival,
Survival means cleaning toilets, flipping burgers
Those jobs you do not want,
But taunt them that do.
Whereas if you were sick while visiting their homelands.
They'd treat you and you'd be glad

Times we live, we don't forgive,
We blame and shame and take for granted
And vote for them that shamefully support the rich
And bitch about, whatever the red tops say
Today
Tomorrow and tomorrow and tomorrow.

Fin Hall, International Beat Poet Laureate, is the New Pitsligo-based poet and ar- s-c organiser extraordinaire. Fin is the host of Like A Blot From The Blue, a poetry and spoken-word event transcending the boundaries of the physical and digital welcoming in hundreds of crea-ves from across the globe as well as a semi regular open mic night at various venues in Aberdeen, Scotland. ..Fin is a profoundly experienced poet with a career spanning decades. On-stage, Fin performs with a beau-ful sensi-vity. He isn't afraid to broach upon themes of old age, hope, love, and loss but reserves a potent and fiery aJtude against injus-ce. Fin is also a filmmaker, collabora-ve writer, performance poet and, publisher. He now co-produces Poetry In The Park, Aberdeen's only monthly outdoor spoken word event, with Birgit Itse. Has been published in over 40  collec-ons, both in print and online from Australia, China, Canada, Pakistan, Nepal, Wales, India, Ireland, England, USA, as well as Scotland. He is also a filmmaker with 10 films of varying length made over the past few years. He loves collabora-ng with other writers and musicians.

নারীর ভূমিকা,

নারী তুমি সবেতেই রাখো ভূমিকা, আরেকটু বুঝলে সবেতেই সেরা।
তুমি মমতাময়ী মায়ায় মেখে রাখো সংসার,
তোমার সাজানো জগতে চলে তোমার উপর ধাঁধা, বাঁধা ও অত্যাচার,
ভেবো দেখো তোমার হাতেই আছে সমাধান।
যুগের পরিবর্তনে তুমি হয়েছো দামী,
সময়ের সাথে যুদ্ধ করে ছিনিয়ে নিয়েছো নিজের অধিকার খানি।
বুঝিয়ে দিয়েছো যুদ্ধে তুমিও পারদর্শী।
পারো এগিয়ে যেতে জয়ের জয়ধ্বনি দিতে।
দক্ষতা রাখো সবেতেই –
"পড়াশোনা, পেশা, প্রযুক্তিবিদ্যা, খেলাধুলা, সংস্কৃতি ও রাজনীতিতে"
সবেতেই থেকো দাপিয়ে ও কাঁপিয়ে।
কম যাওনা কোনো কিছুতে, তাহলে কিসের ভয়!
ভয় ত্যাগ করো, শক্ত হও।
এই রাত তোমার, এই সমাজ তোমার, স্বাধীনতাও তোমার।
তোমার রাজত্বে অন্য কেন থাবা দেয়!
প্রসারিত ও বিকশিত রাতকে কেন অন্যের হাতের মুঠে দাও!
তুমি মা তুমি পারো "শেখাতে নারীদের শ্রদ্ধা ও সম্মান করতে",
তোমার শিক্ষার মাধ্যমে তুমি পারো "নারী জগতের পরিবর্তন করতে"
"নারী জগতের আলোড়ন করতে"।

PRIYANKA NEOGI

ROLE OF WOMEN

Women, you just keep your role,
if you understand a little more, it's the best.
You cover the world with compassion,
Riddles, fetters, and tortures pervade you
in your arranged world,
Look, you have the solution.
You have become precious in the change of era,
You have taken away your rights by fighting against time.
You have explained that you are also good at war.
May you go ahead and give a shout of victory.
Just keep the skills –
"In education, profession, technology, sports, culture and politics"
Just stay strong and tremble.
Don't go short in anything, so what's the fear!
Leave fair, keep strong.
This night is yours, this society is yours,
your freedom is your hand.
Why else paws in your kingdom!
Why give the extended and developed night
in the hands of others!
You mother you can "teach to respect and honor to women,"
You can "change the world of women" through your education,
"To stir the world of women."

Amb. Dr. Priyanka Neogi is from India. She is a business women, librarian, teacher, International poet, Story writer, Author, columnist, Researcher, Editor, Live telecaster, Translator, cultural enthusiast, Acting, dancer, singer, reciter, n.s.s, host, anchor, judges, Keynote speaker, literacy organizer international field, Ambassador, social worker, National Joint Secretary UAP Miss India 2nd Runner's up 2022, Vogue Star Miss India official candidate of 2024. Journalist an International literary editor, Founder Kalpanar Kabita Sahitya Samajik and Sangskritik Parishad of India, Indian President of Comilla Kabi Parishad of Bangladesh. She is multi-talented and versatile. She is a national and international awardee.

PRENDETE UN POVERO CRISTO

Prendete un povero cristo
e gettatelo tra le mascelle di un tornio
oppure tra i denti di una fresa
da mattina fino a sera
tutto il giorno gobbo a stringere il lavoro
guardatelo come impazzisce e si consuma
quanta schiuma gli sale in corpo
e aspettate poi che esca dalla fabbrica
per vedere dove sfoghi la rabbia
se nelle relazioni sociali
oppure a tavola su moglie e figli
chiudetelo in un buco di reparto
e spiatelo
a ciondolare a uccidersi di noia
a perdere pezzi mentre i minuti cadono
a spegnersi con il determinato
senza dargli conferme per il futuro
prendete il suddetto ex uomo
e chiamatelo maiale
e tenetelo stretto per il collo
vediamo se non stacca gli occhi dal lavoro
vediamo se non vi incendia
una volta dentro al vostro cazzo di ufficio

Take a Poor Guy

Take a poor guy
and throw him between the jaws of a lathe
or between the teeth of a milling machine
from morning till night
all day hunched over to his work
watch him going crazy and wearing himself out
how much foam rises in his body
and then wait for him to leave the factory
to see where he takes his anger out
if on social relationships
or at the table on his wife and children
lock him in a dump department
and spy on him
hanging around killing himself with boredom
losing pieces while the minutes tick by
burning out with a temporary contract
without providing him security for the future
take the aforementioned ex-man
and call him pig
and hold him tight by the neck
let's see if he doesn't take his eyes off his work
let's see if he doesn't set you on fire
once inside your fucking office

Matteo Rusconi was born in Lodi (Italy) in 1979. He currently teaches in a technical institute and has worked as a turner, milling machine operator and sandblaster. In 2021 he published *Trucioli*, a collection of poems in which he recounts the life in a factory and its alienations. Several of his poems appear in many anthologies of contemporary poetry and they have been translated for some foreign magazines.

Waking Up

I asked the French press for coffee,
hoping to start my morning
in a civilized manner, a little
common ground
or lingua franca served in a little cup
made to sip rather than gulp,
no room
for milk or cream or sugar
because such additives
dilute the stormy richness and rightness
of coffee made black and
strong. And the French press

turned up their noses,
shuffled their berets,
smoked clove cigarettes on
darkened street corners,
bemoaning the ails of
society, the depravity
of drive thru coffee, or good
morning spoken in any language
other than French.

They wrote it in bold
headlines, then went
on strike, then went on
holiday, then swore
a lot, stamped out their
cigarettes, mopped
their brows, swore off philosophy
until tomorrow, made their own coffee,
worked late in to the night
to make deadline –
I think tomorrow I'll have a
cup of tea.

A time traveling arsonist, **John Reinhart** writes in ashes by candlelight. Editor of *Star*Line and *winner* of the Horror Writers Association Dark Poetry Scholarship, Reinhart writes poetry ranging from heartfelt to heart-wrenching to robots in space with no hearts. He manages the Poetry Across Maine project – an oral history/documentary self-guided tour of Maine through poetry.

My Mother's Hands

Hard-boiled eggs
my mother peeled
with calloused fingers, chipped
nails, protruding veins
– mycelia.
Salmon nail plate, back bent,
bent over backwards for me, always
me & my 2-hour commute & my
fatherlessness. I missed
the bus already. I beg
those spiderlegs to spin
the web of my lunch faster.
Egg cradled, gently.
Pearl.

Always late,
never hungry.

Alejandra C. Chavez

ON HOME ECONOMICS

My mother with the food stamps.
My mother at the bus stop with four children.
Somehow fed us. Roof
over our heads leased,
five in a studio apartment.

We got luxuries like toothpaste and lotion (as a kid,
in Jalisco, my mother's skin crinkled like a paper bag)
and when the lotion emptied, she cut through round plastic
with 99 cent store scissors, and when the toothpaste
gave out, she rolled the bottom upward –
squeezed out another week.

My brother got Converse or Vans – his pick.
I got a Kovu & Kiara purse at Payless
and a pair of flip-flops.

There was always something to buy; Keep
household afloat.
Somehow, always, she stretched a dollar.
We had beans and *confléis* and sopas de agua,
clear gel for my brother's spiky hair, for me: a mermaid
electric toothbrush, bus pass with my picture on it, a passport,
garage sale Barbies – dozens of them, Mattel convertible
(gently used).

If you had told me we were poor,
I wouldn't have believed it.

Alejandra C. Chavez earned her MFA in Poetry from the University of California Riverside. She earned her Bachelor's Degree at Kalamazoo College, where she majored in Anthropology and Sociology, but sneaked in enough English classes to receive an English minor. Upon graduating, Alejandra left the mitten state to return home to Los Angeles, where she worked with youth ages 6-18 at 826LA's After-School Writing & Tutoring Program. She is the author of the children's book "My Bestie the Crestie," which hopes to inspire love and respect for reptiles and other creatures. Alejandra's poetry has been published in About Place Journal, Nighthawk Literature, Vitni Review, Mujeres de Maíz, Hinchas de Poesia, and East Jasmine Review. She currently lives in Los Angeles with her nine crested geckos and her spunky maltipoo named Boba.

I Am Not Tongva*

No, I am not Tongva
but they are everywhere.
From Malibu to Azusa
"E'kwa'shem" echoes, **"We are still here."**

Though I am not Tongva
I walk their ancient paths.
As I gather acorns under oak trees
I sense that this is still their land.

Their footprints are found across Los Angeles
But to them this was **Yaagna**.
Stand still with me a moment
and you will hear the shaman's holy song.

Soon a hawk circles above me.
I imagine it calls my name.
Notion of time dissolves into nothing.
Past and present become the same.

Suddenly there are no skyscrapers
or even the ruins of adobe walls.
There are only Tule huts along a riverbank
and the blackest night of brilliant starts.

So, I know that I am not Tongva
but I know that they're still here.
E'kwa'shem resonates through the canyon
that they are present. They are near.

* *The Tongva are the indigenous people of the Los Angeles basin area. Azusa and Malibu are the names of former villages as are Topanga and Cahuenga.*

Victor Avila is a winner of the Chicano Literary Prize. He is a poet, songwriter, and illustrator. Victor's poetry has been widely published and anthologized. Recent work can be found in such collections as EXTREME: An Anthology for Social and Economic Justice and The Border Crossed Us. Roots-rock hero Dave Alvin has called Victor "the real king of California" for his songwriting. He has one album, Crow on the Cradle, available through CD Baby and a second one will be released later this year. Victor also writes and illustrates the comic book series Hollywood Ghost Comix. He is currently at work on his first graphic novel, The Night of the Obsidian Blade. Victor has taught in California public schools for almost thirty years.

EXPOSED

The hard black nightstick explodes into my back.
One thump feels like a thousand punches.
All these cops descending on me and for what?

I'm acting out over the oppression that continues to slap me.

My memory floats back to 1990 and Rodney King.
How in the hell did he survive that beating?
Our ancestors survived a hundred times worse.

I'm watching all these troupes of injustice still invading my soul.

Today they make it quick and just shoot you.
Those bullets don't ask any questions.
They answer by ripping your humanity away.

I'm thinking outside the box as I sit in a cell and piss away my future.

Running from demons who chase the air I breathe.
Crying after every nightmare praying for a dream to cleanse my spirit.
Being a productive human being was too much to ask.

I'm loving nothing and have no one to love.

I sued LAPD and they took a deposition on what happened.
I didn't know what that word meant or trust the system.
I guess my lawyer was going to help me or help himself.

I slip into darkness, unconsciousness, and confusion.

I screamed out to my brother.
                    Mother
                    Father
                    Sister

No one answered, called, or cared unless I got paid.

My ashes got tossed into the trash.

My memory is not worth a quarter- Exposed.

WOODROW BAILEY

THE FIFTH

The South LA morning sun heats up my tired body.
The ashy skin has not been washed in a year.
The few teeth that didn't divorce my mouth hurt.

This all adds up to a homeless, helpless and a heritage of havoc.

I'm not considered employable.
I'm not measured by your standards.
I'm not etched in stone by any god.

That all subtracts to a useless soul to be used.

When you drive by my raggedy, mix mashed blue tent.
When you cringe at the thought I am headed towards your car.
When you can't walk on the sidewalk because of the stench.

Those points divide the haves from the have nots without race, creed, or color.

I see the same Los Angeles as you do.
I see cultures living and breathing in harmony with hope.
I see how gentrification is an affordable housing nightmare.

These views multiply the blatant disrespect by omission.

Politicians keep promising to house the homeless.
Politicians are winds of change as they taste greed.
Politicians lie as easy as they breathe.

Where does that math leave me?

It's senseless to think my situation will get any better.
It's sensible to believe this America will not help us.
It's made sense to document these atrocities.

I plead the fifth as I drink it down slowly.

Woodrow Bailey was born New Orleans and raised in South Central Los Angeles. His creativity took flight when his mother taught him how to read and write at age three. His philanthropy, his career, and his writing represent those with no voice or choice in this society. Woodrow Bailey uses the commodity of words as a prose into his environment; he sees those who are left with little to no option as his audience. His writing is their testimony as he observes social issues. As the same streets he grew up on continue to be his composition book, those life lessons fuel what he stands for: Peace and Faith.

THE WORD 'COMRADE' TASTES LIKE BREAD

The word 'comrade' tastes like bread
like blood
like sisterhood brotherhood
like the hand reaching out
or the shovel to the soil –
the word 'comrade' sings in my mouth
with an arm around yr shoulder
and tears over the grave –

The word 'comrade' reaches the sky
as fist to the air
or a tree reaching tall
because roots matter more.
And yet the word the name 'comrade' is going out of fashion
just as we need it most.

But I love you, comrade.
Come, take my hand.
And pass the message along.
There's work to be done
and vampires in the hall;
the workers must eat today
and taste the milk of freedom
even if it's only in our dreams
as our song is passed along
and the name the word, is heard again.

Karlostheunhappy, born in Wales but now hiding in the dark Forest of Dean, England, is a writer inspired by the Beat Generation, Brautigan, Basho and Blake as well as Dylan Thomas and ee cummings among others. His work has featured in Beatdom and IT (international times) and numerous anthologies. He is the author of OBLIVION: 200 Seasons (of pain and magic) through Gloomy for Pleasure press. He was editor at underground 90s litzine BeatSurreal, for which he's working on a best-of and new anthology for Gloomy for Pleasure (expected 2025). He worked with Portland poet and houseless activist Mimi German on Flowers of the Litter, an anthology that included George Wallace, Fred Voss and Bill Lewis among homeless street poets, with Karlostheunhappy editing snippets of Whitman throughout the text. The collection was recently previewed at the Walt Whitman Birthplace Museum. Karlostheunhappy also spoke at Oxford Blackwell's on Jack Kerouac and suffering to mark the Kerouac centenary and sat on the editorial committee for the Wye Valley & Forest of Dean Clarion magazine, an independent political paper. A former CP member, now navigating his life towards secular Buddhism, he's a long-time CND member and has been involved in many different progressive campaigns over the years.

LICKETY SPLIT

"r > g"
Thomas Piketty
Capital in the Twenty-First Century

Piketty Piketty
lickety splittety

r > g:
returns on capital will grow faster than the economy

That is,
for those who are economically challenged:

the fat cats grow fatter
while the 99.99% go hungry

Piketty Piketty
lickety splittety

It's the speed of green:
the more you got the more you get
and the faster you get it

Lickety split:
trust fund babies
goo goo gaa gaa
lifestyles of the rich and libidinous

("Feds investigating Massachusetts, Virginia brothel network seek
charges against 28 alleged clients" *Boston Globe* Dec 18, 2023)

and we watch through the windows of our televisions
like the homeless outside five-star restaurants

Like starting on third base and thinking you've hit a homerun
but not Chuck Collins
grandson of Oscar Mayer
hot dog
gave his inheritance away now fights against inequality

or Nick Hanauer
who admits in his TED talk
called "The dirty secret of capitalism"
how the filthy rich get filthier

Like playing Monopoly

but one percent starts with hotels on Boardwalk
and 99 start with nothing:
we don't have a chance in hell.
Call me snowball
snowball poet shouting out loud:

read a book
read piketty

Go ahead, Google it:
debt snowball vs. debt avalanche

Piketty Piketty
lickety splittety

goo goo gaa gaa
daddy gave me $400 million
I was a landlord at three years old
goo goo gaa gaa

("How Donald Trump's Father Made Him a Landlord at Age 3" *New York Times* Oct 3, 2018)

The true scandal of Cattelan's "Comedian"
– you know, the Duchampian banana duct-taped to the wall
("the now infamous spoof of art-world capitalism" *Washington Post* Nov 24, 2024)
– is that there was a room full of people bidding millions for it:
"disposable income"

Meanwhile
disposable people
homeless houseless have-nots
holding out the jingle-cup
and hurricane victims in western Carolina
afraid to take help from FEMA

A snowball's chance in hell
and I am the snowball poet
absolute zero of an influencer
– influence relies on flow
and this river is frozen stiff
like the lake around Satan in Dante's *Inferno*
Cocytus

Fight fire with fire?
Fight fire with snowballs
99 snowballs
rolling toward hell

packed tight with stones with boulders
the rolling stone gathers no moss

but an avalanche?
Now that's something

Richard Smyth has previously been anthologized
by Vagabond Books in *Extreme* (2018), *Dissent*
(2023), and *The Vagabond Lunar Collection*
(2025). Similar work is anthologized in *Liberty's
Vigil: The Occupy Anthology: 99 Poets Among the
99%* (Foothills Publishing, 2013) and *Winter in
America Again* (Carbonation Press, 2025). He is
editor and publisher of the environmental poetry
journal *Albatross*, which started in 1986. He
holds a Ph.D. in English from the University of
Florida and currently lives in Krakow, Poland.

DECLINE RULES THE HORIZON

There are no lessons to be learned from arid acres that surround,
empty lanes that parallel tracks of box cars, funeral cars.
I lapse into sarcasm.
It's what I do since
I don't believe in truth, closure, Jesus.
Through weeks of corner shadows,
songs learned from the marketplace –
Caligula's orgy arias,
Bonaparte's melodies for peace,
are all I know to sing.

Raised by complaint, lost in years leashed by past battles,
I read *The Crucifixion Diary* every year;
make circumstance another habit to obey.
In reading, those results translate as:
"No God, only worshippers."
Down a sunblind street –
Dead Flowers on repeat,
Dodge Dually ripping surface roads,
I center routines where salutations
of deceit are formed for posts of posthumous regards.
"You are my undeserved conscience," one friend writes.

Raking distrust, flag grievances, lost privilege as motives,
The Copperhead Agenda is in motion.
Resolution is *Facebook Reels* of Strother Martin muttering
disaster into Warren Oates' ear, the scent and smoke swirl of
lemon trees burning across skyscraper windows.
Laying my head down, I try to remember your face
alive in weeks less bitter,
places more specific.
Weary of death but
not of war,
I can't.

R.T. Castleberry, a Pushcart Prize nominee, has work in
Sangam, Glassworks, Gyroscope Review, Silk Road, and
StepAway. Internationally, he's had poetry published in
Canada, Wales, Ireland, Scotland, France, New Zealand,
Portugal, the Philippines, India and Antarctica. His poetry
has appeared in the anthologies: You Can Hear the
Ocean: An Anthology of Classic and Current Poetry,
TimeSlice, The Weight of Addition, and Level Land: Poetry
For and About the I35 Corridor.

Marriage Vow

One country is not the world. I missed the moon this morning.
Only a film-softened face. Dawn. My old house in the woods became
a meth lab. How can that be? That healing place where poetry
found me wandering the woods.
Today's sky white, someone said that is the weight of snow.
The Arctic melts. Loosening bergs desalinate the sea. Their sighs die,
high summer, winter falls on us all at once.
No fairy tale, Earth's aridification.
No fairytale winter this.
Sunset. Wild fires. Today we remember a peace-making murdered man.
Where is hell? Dancing in Los Angeles? Flames. I wonder where the
angels are, the heroes. That murdered man thanked darkness for
revealing stars. Grab one, starlight pierces your palm, you bleed.
Don't let go. With your other hand reach for your neighbor's.
Make a ring. Big enough, tight enough to marry an entire planet.

RESISTING

I type poems at the kitchen table
to resist despair. Glue
wings on each stanza, every line,
listen, their voices'

background song like birds or insects
in a movie, their fragrance a snowy
petrichor that washes my hair back
from my face

when I open the window.
Winter gusts take them, but it was me,
who could've clung, their stilled
wings folded in a closet with bars.
My hands released. A closet is no place
for wings.

Rachael Ikins is a multiple Pushcart nominee, 2018 Independent Book Award winner, 2024 winner 2nd place Northwind Writing Awards, activist author/artist of 13 books. Her cats and dogs remain unimpressed with this and will sit on the keyboard if she works past their mealtimes. Her artwork has appeared in NYC, Paris, France and Washington DC. Syracuse University grad, member Bayou City branch NLAPW, and Associate Editor of Clare Songbirds Publishing House, Auburn, NY

MALASANA

You pay extra to sit outside
And watch the evening passers-by.
Sip coffee, beer, enjoy the crowd
And never share your thoughts aloud.
These streets as well have known their flights
As demonstrators hymned the night,
Their flags and banners scald the air
As sirens keen and rockets flare.
This square once filled with chants and songs,
That fleeting sense that we belong,
The contact point of fear and dreams
Played out in memory's flickering scenes.
These revolutions ebb and fail
As round the longing streets I trail,
A wanderer between the wars
And not sure what's worth fighting for.
The young men scorn my holding back
And value doubts less than attack.
But trembling hands aren't always fear
Regret and shame are rioting here.
Is hope just one thrown brick away
As tear gas wafts and flames display
The power of words to make us think
We are immortal, on the brink
Of better times, justice and peace.
With shields and batons come police
Still more young braves so proud and scared
They dare not stop – so be prepared
For fighting and for quick arrests.
Real men stand up for these cruel tests,
Their strength is not to walk away
But make their news in bold display
While poets wonder, can't decide
If paint and slogans make a side
Or are they servants of our hands
Instructed by cool, wise commands.
Maybe words scurry out of sight
And freed, they set the world alight.

Peter Appleton has worked in theatre, education and campaigning. He's lived and worked in several countries, now based in the UK, investigating where the personal meets the political.

THE LIGHTNING STORMS OF VENUS

And now, what do I have to show for it?
A few folk tale motifs,
oracles and spectral visions,
cobwebs of sacred inebriations –
the forgotten lightning strike of love-at-first-sight
from the little Golden Age of my youth –
Now I know it's called *limerence,*
a garden-variety mental disturbance.

Nonetheless, I fondly remember
the reckless rush of ecstasy
on Saturday all-night dance parties –
Carefree, Pleasuredome, Club Universe –
where working class gay men and women
could blow off some proletarian steam
under the auspices of ancient cosmologies
and astral declinations,
deep fugitive feelings,
irrational soul stirrings
like a wild pilgrimage into untrammeled nature
far away from the work-a-day world
of pecking orders
and cold caffeinated reason.

As golden years approach
(fatigue settling into my bones)
what happened to all of that inspiration?
I'm amazed I once could feel that deeply
for my auburn muse of the day,
my cool male Venus?
Even if it was a misguided limerence,
where did those all-consuming fires
of passion go?

Fallen Adonnais!
Reply to us like Alien Gods
in the lightning storms
of Venus!

***

Somewhere in that convoluted timeline,
in those universal primate feelings of *eros* of *agape* –
flashing turbulently from time-to-time like
the lightning storms of Venus.

Ahhh! Foolish youthful
ecstasy filling me like
an empty vessel elevating me
to rarefied states of being
high above fractal things below –
then bringing me down hard
again to pick up the pieces
before a blue Monday morning.

Here, in the artificial beauty
of this sleek transparent tower,
Adonnais is silent Now,
sending no oracles of love or
even fragmented text messages
from the Great Beyond.

***

Was it even real to begin with?
A woven shared fantasy?
Or just proof of a world of delusion,
as the Buddhists claim?
The product of imbalanced neurochemistry
buried at unsounded depths
in folds of a waxy brain
close to secret sub-zones
where I can imagine such strange things as
the lightning storms of Venus?

(deep breathing)

More rational now.
I throw myself into
the daily cubist routine –
a small wheel turning inside
bigger wheels of macro-economics,
rededicating myself to the *task-at-hand*.

– Unsigned

Ron Myers wrote his first poems at Indiana University in the 1970s. In San Francisco, Ron workshopped his poems with Harold Norse, Neeli Cherkovski and Clive Matson. His subjects include environmental causes, ancient world cultures, geography (exterior/interior), and love and its frustrations. Ron was recently appointed the National Beat Poetry Foundation's Poet Laureate for California for 2024-2026. His poems have appeared in The Slant, The Scribbler, Beatdom, The Brooklyn Rail and over a dozen anthologies in the U.S., England, France and Italy.

ALTROVE

Ondoso meticcio   litoraneo grosso sasso montuoso
mostruoso prende a schiaffi   ombra   a distanza di passo
fortuito e palleggio   pallone numero molten aperitivo per
cane essere umano monge   essere umano a volte e sulla schiena
s'atteggia sudore saetta fetore   languore interstizi zecche nascoste
negli orifizi   secche di conchiglie   pericolose come stoviglie
arrugginite ste figlie appese al mondo   vettovaglie arrese
all'ultimo soffio di solleone all'ultima stazione   all'ultima
canzone che parte al contrario   senza preavviso   ci senti una voce
ma è solo il tuo peso   è solo il tuo viso   se lasci un'impronta
sul bagnasciuga che importa   se resta il contorno   la linea
d'ombra è solo un avviso   ti dice dividi pure il pane con gli
sconosciuti   bevi la stessa acqua dove bevono prostitute e detenuti
dove corrono cavalle il mare diventa oceano   diventa solo una
linea   da oltrepassare diventa solo che   dall'altra parte c'è
dimmelo pure se sto bruciando vivo non ci sono specchi qui vicino
non posso guardarmi   posso solo dimmelo pure se   oltre la
linea del dove non c'è nulla   di più di un salto nel   dimmelo
pure se vuoi puoi venire con me   ma solo in caso tu fossi
altrove tu fossi realmente decisamente   solo una cosa che muore.

STEFANO TARQUINI

ELSEWHERE

Wavy coastal mongrel   large mountainous rock
monstrous slaps   shadow   at the distance
fortuitous step   and ball dribble   molten number aperitif for
a dog human being monge   human being sometimes on the back
it poses sweat lightning stench   languor interstices ticks hidden
in the orifices   shoals of shells   dangerous like rusty dishes
these daughters hanging out   the world   provisions surrendered
to the last breath of sun at the last station   at the last song that starts
backwards   without warning   you hear a voice
but it's only your weight   it's only your face   if you leave a footprint on
the shoreline what does it matter   if the outline remains   the shadow
line is only a warning   it tells you go ahead and share your bread with
strangers   drink the same water where prostitutes and prisoners
drink where mares run the sea becomes an ocean   becomes only a
line to cross   becomes only that   on the other side there is   tell me
even if I'm burning alive there are no mirrors nearby   I can't look at
myself   I can only tell me   even if beyond the line of where there is
nothing more   than a leap in tell me even if you want you can come
with me   but only in case you were   elsewhere you were
really definitely   just a thing that dies.

Stefano Tarquini was born in Rome on June 28, 1978, and lives in Guidonia. He is a literary talent scout at Read(y), poetry editor at Super Tramps Club, creator and host of the poetry festival Argini and the streaming format on Italian poetry Sourpoetry. He is the voice of the post core band Palkosceniko al Neon and the voice of the spoken word band L'Amorte. In August 2021 his first collection of poems "I giorni furiosi" was released with Transeuropa. "Cucina vigliacca" was released in October 2024 with Giulio Perrone editore, and it's his second collection.

Another Day in Life.

HR called me and told me I need to come at 2pm
Bring your union rep. That's what she said

I called her back and said I couldn't find a rep for 2pm
When can you get a rep then?

I told her 3pm.
That's fine. Looking forward to meeting with you.

But, I don't understand why she called for a meeting.

No, I can't remember any problems with my work.

I'm trying not to worry but I'm worried
HR doesn't just call for no reason.

Maybe she's going to help me prepare for retirement?
Does HR do that?

I don't know either. Yes, Brian is the rep who's coming.

Yeah, Brian's a good man.
He has helped me before.

That time I was in trouble for being out sick a few months ago.
Yeah, the time my grandson Ronnie was so sick.

They said I was misusing my sick time.
I was supposed to apply for a leave or something.
They always have some form to fill out.

There was that other time, I almost forgot.
I had to leave to get Ronnie from day care.
They are really strict about picking him up on time.

Well, I told my supervisor Marcie that day that I couldn't stay over.

Yeah, It was my turn on the overtime list.
I did try to find somebody to take my place.

Yeah the supervisor Marcie was pissed she had to stay instead.
But that was over a year ago now.

You know, Marcie's been out for me ever since.
She's always checking if I get back from break on time

Yeah, I know it's her job.

But it's not like I'm always late.
Taking care of Ronnie in the mornings runs me down
He's just 3 now. You know they have all that energy.

That's why I fall asleep on breaks.
I've told Marcie that I take care of Ronnie

What about my daughter Sharon?

You know she's trying to keep off the meth.

She tries. She was in rehab again a few months back.

No, Sharon doesn't get a steady paycheck.
She really can't.
She hangs out with that guy Jerry.
He's the bad one; got her started on the meth.

Yeah, so I really need the money I get from this job.
You know how kids eat, new clothes, plus my rent and all…

Right, Oooops, Brian's here already. Call you back.

I'm so happy to see you again, Shirley.

She was so nice and smiling.

Sit down. Would you like some water?

I was so surprised. Brian said afterward he was suspicious.

Your supervisor and I have been reviewing your performance lately.
She mentions how you've not been doing your assignments.
She's shown me all the evaluations and work plans.
You signed that you read them and understood you needed to improve.

Well, yes Marcie's been meeting with me. I thought she met with everyone.
Brian looked over the papers. He gave them back.
He explained to the HR woman that I'd had many family and personal issues.

I'm sorry about that. But her supervisor followed the procedures.
She was given performance review plans which she didn't follow.

I told you before Marcie was out to get me.

Of course, I did what I could to follow the plans.
I told the HR woman about that.
I try to do some work for the other staff too.

I'm sorry, this is very hard to tell you.
We're going to have to let you go.
Security will take you back to your station.
You can pick up your personal belongings.
I'm handing you the notice and we are extending a severance package.
4 weeks is what we give in these circumstances.

Four weeks! How am I gonna get a job in four weeks?

She said that I wouldn't be able to collect unemployment.

Yeah, because I'm not being laid off.
Brian said they'd try to get them to change this.
Maybe he can get them to lay me off instead.

Yeah, Brian told me not to get my hopes up.

I'm sorry we had to meet under these circumstances, Shirley.
Security is here for you now.

I just needed two more years before I could retire.

Stephen Iannaccone is a current resident of Swampscott, MA where he resides with his spouse, Greg Getschman. Stephen was named Poet Laureate of Swampscott for 2015. Stephen grew up and studied in Boston, MA at Boston Latin School, St, John Seminary College and Northeaster University with an MPA degree. He lived for 25 years in Somerville, MA. In the past, he was a frequent visitor to Provincetown. He worked for the Fernald Center in Waltham for 23 years before retirement. His publications include *Atlantic Anthology, Cooch Behar Anthology Vol. 3 and Short Stories, Vol. 2* all published by Cooch Behar Press. In April, 2025, his book *A Mystical State of Reason* is scheduled be published by Vagabond.

We Said We Were the Poem & Became the Meme

That's when I realized
our mission is utter insanity

Again.

In a car I trust
in cities – now barreling
no guardrails
Wyoming

Burning oil & rubber, of course
we get a nail in the tire

Unreliable & ready,
we're prepared
for how unprepared we are

Our cause is holier than your laws
& rifles thru your sock drawer
searching for lil orange pills. Justification
is for people who don't know how to tell the truth
& I'm all out of excuses.

There's one more crossroads to bear –
I guess I'll be honest this time:
let my family know
I'm having the time of my life.

Everything is fire
& the smoke spells Freedom™

If we are the poem,
we are inked with blood & oil,
war machine run off,
the gaudy myths of men
who did great things & we
are doing great things. Look
a traditional madness:
rushing cliffs for fortunes,
ruin breathing sweetly
on your neck

Out in the Rockies
where the predators pray,
where desire sings
in the key of calories,
I sip cucumber gatorade
& so sweetly neuter the tune

Chicago –
we put our faith in the lost & found,
where the rats look both ways
before crossing the street

In Denver,
barstool poetica wanders all night,
through streets still aching
from someone else's dream

Yippidity yap goofs in Rapid City,
scheme ourselves west
while Yale professors
catch flights to Europe

We can't afford to run –
so come drowning,
we crave our last breaths
climbing black into blue,
bubbles yearning yellow-white
break surface
pop
& everyone will go
Ooooooo
& Ahhhhh
they never said a commonplace thing
Ooooo
Ahhhh

My ex my girl my liminal space
where the lil boy in my heart sighs with relief
She chews me out
when I said
I'm going to be a legend.

Darling,
legends don't write their own stories.

* from "Holistic Hooligans," a split chap with Damian Rucci
published by MadCap Press

Jeremiah Walton doesn't trust bios, but still wants you to
know he's the founder of the spectacle that is Bards On The
Rocks, traveling bookstore Books & Shovels, & Nostrovia!
Press, & an alumni of the Osage Arts Community. People
have moshed to his poems. Once, he read from the center
of the pit. Nobody heard him, but what a great time. After
12,000 miles on the 2025 Vagabond Poetry Tour, he is
upholding the millennial tradition of concluding his 20s by
moving back in with mom. Catch him writing about his
years on the road at jeremiahwalton.substack.com +
cyberbullying poets on IG @cancelpoetry

WISE HOPE

Aching world, I see you,
where wars scar the soil,
and injustice wears heavy boots.
Hope feels like a frail whisper,
trembling beneath the shadow of despair.
Why bother?
Why cradle the fragile flame
when storms howl so loudly?
Ordinary hope, they call it,
a desperate thread of desire,
clinging to what cannot be held.
But wise hope –
it is the quiet inhale before action,
the steadfast gaze into the heart of suffering,
the certainty that meaning persists,
even when outcomes dissolve
into the unknowable mist.
Wise hope does not dream of gardens
while standing in ash.
It stands in ash,
and plants seeds anyway,
trusting the rain, the soil,
the shift of seasons we cannot command.
It knows that uncertainty
is not an enemy,
but a spacious field where change grows.
Show up.
Two words carved into the temple of being.
Face the 65 million displaced souls,
the forests crumbling into sand,
the oceans rising like an unanswered question.
Show up for the bedside vigil,
the ballot box,
the breaking moment
when humanity falters,
yet finds its footing again.
Wise hope does not flee the present,
nor does it adorn it with false light.
It bows to impermanence,
to the inevitable turning
of every wheel and tide.
It breathes where apathy cannot,
moves where fear stills.
It trusts in the unseen ripples
of even the smallest act.

Stasha Powell is an Ohio (by way of SF)
gothic poet and creative writer with a flair
for the macabre. Her work often explores
themes of darkness, transformation, and
empowerment. Currently pursuing a
degree in Creative Writing with a
concentration in Poetry at SNHU, Stasha
channels her unique perspective into
powerful, emotionally resonant pieces.

THE FALL OF CROWNS

The throne was never solid,
it was always a house of cards,
built on the breath of yes-men
and the silence of the afraid.
But now, the wind shifts.
An undertone becomes a roar,
and the scepter slips
from fingers too weak to hold it.
The crown, that gilded lie,
rolls across the floor,
its jewels winking like the eyes of traitors.
And the king?
He is already a ghost,
his shadow is dissolving
into the cracks of the marble.
The people do not cheer.
They do not weep.
They simply turn their faces
to the sun,
as if they had forgotten
it could shine.

CHRISTIAN EMECHETA

THE UNMAKING OF A TITAN

They came for him at dawn,
when the sky was still bleeding
the colors of night.
He stood tall, like
a colossus carved from arrogance,
his eyes fixed on a distance
he could no longer reach.
But the ground beneath him
was already crumbling,
the earth reclaiming its own.
One by one,
the pillars of his power fell,
each crash a stamp of ruin.
And when the dust settled,
there was nothing left
but the sound of his breath,
shallow and ambiguous,
as if he were learning
how to be human again.

Christian Emecheta is a writer, illustrator, and Computer Scientist. His fiction and poetry have appeared in many online publications and magazines such as Arts Lounge Magazine, Writefluence Anthology, Synchronized Chaos Online Journal, The Decolonial Passage, Mocking Owl Roost, and elsewhere. He write songs whenever he is inspired by a tune or some music lyrics. Christian enjoys reading, watching movies, and getting lost in his imaginations.

At the World War III Museum

Scattered cars in the parking lot
resembling burned popcorn

Shadows of people and dogs
on the scorched building walls

Inside mounds of bone and flesh
as if this was a supermarket

Go out into the Ground Zero
air and never come back again

Don Kingfisher Campbell, MFA Antioch University L.A.,
taught at USC and Occidental College Upward Bound, board
member California Poets In The Schools, publisher Four
Feathers Press, host of the Saturday Afternoon Poetry
reading and workshop series in Pasadena, California. For
awards, features, and publication credits, please go to:
http://dkc1031.blogspot.com

EVOLUTION TO DISSOLUTION

We, the human race, are the handiwork of billions of years of evolution.

Our fragile planet has survived not one, but two global extinctions.

We are the aftermath of those who survived the second one.

We were not around for the great continental drifts that separated Pangea into seven separate continents.

We were not around when the globe was one hundred percent covered in ice, a proverbial global ice ball.

We were not around when the Siberian Flats spewed enough lava that it would have covered what is now North America in a hot liquid magma, three hundred feet deep.

We were not around after the first extinction that eventually resulted in the rising of dinosaurs who lived here for one hundred sixty-five million years and is known as the Mesozoic Era.

We were not around for the second extinction that wiped out not only the dinosaurs, but almost every breath of life itself, except the smallest of mammals who if they had not survived, we would not exist.

Us. Who spread out from the depths of what we now call Africa, and spanned the globe looking for food, shelter, and room to live as our masses expanded over the millennia.

Us. With our larger brains and opposable thumbs took from what the earth provided and found ways of developing food through farming, shelter through logging, and eventually a profound understanding of our world through agriculture, technology, and science.

Us. Having discovered we are now destroying our atmosphere through greenhouse gases eleven times faster than the first extinction when those greenhouse gases, at that time, were caused by massive worldwide volcanic eruptions.

Us. Because so many deniers continue to doubt the science that shows demonstrably how we are quickly approaching the tipping point, evidenced by rising sea temperatures, melting glaciers, more frequent violent storms, and the highest global temperatures on record.

Us. Who will be responsible for our own global extinction and that of almost every species on early as we destroy our very fragile atmosphere as thick in relation to the earth, as is the skin on an apple.

But never fear. The earth has proved over and over and over again that it will survive. It will rebound. It will repair itself. It will bring forth new life that will thrive and evolve and produce a whole new range of species, some of whom may never have existed before. And it will do it all without Us.

 **Lee Moss** is a poet and nature photographer. His poetry covers the gamut from humor to social justice. His inspirations comes from the world we live in, how we treat it and how we treat each other. He is also an accomplished photographer, often combining his passion for photography and poetry, writing verse that add a third dimension to his photos. He is also currently working on his first novel.

THE WILDCAT IN THE BURGER SHOP

It was at the place where they put bible verses
on the bottom of their cups and packaging.
I listened to a lot of early Dropkick Murphy's,
Elliott Smith, taking pills as my mouth fell out
a piece at a time waiting on benefits to happen.
Boss said I was going to be in his management program.
But I must have given the wrong co-workers rides.
They all seemed to be the passed over
for promotion people with limited hours
and suck schedules, it was when I purposed
that instead of training the people who
hadn't worked there long and end up leaving
a week or two later that they train the core workers,
show up on time workers, work workers.
I wasn't even necessarily talking about the me worker.
Well, that must had been the last straw
though the company had millions.
My hours got cut, days got fucked.
When I asked to be reimbursed (per policy)
for driving to other locations for supplies
they offered to get someone else to do it.
I shut up because driving meant I could squeeze
I in extra smokes the same reason I'd volunteer
to empty the trash compactor, hoisting that
heavy cube of garbage with a select fellow
smoker co-worker listen, solidarity
isn't In-N-Out It's always.
I was raised by a Hoffa Teamster.
My send-out from a union hall was in the waning days
of car bomb Culinary local 226. Now my name was
prefilled out on write-up forms and that was when
I went to work against work
stealing uniforms to sell online, hiding aprons,
mixing up name badges, and losing hats.
I memorized the prices + tax of all items.
I rang customers up without ringing them up.
I taught other underappreciated workers my system.
We made up for our lost wages and then some.
There was an inventory loss meeting every week.
Whatever measure they came up with
I found a work-around. We affected automated voices
when working the drive through. Told customers
you didn't just have to call it animal style.
You could call it dolphin style, mammal style,
doggy style with the sloppy sauce.
What management thought they knew, they couldn't prove.

We looked out for each other the best we could.

Inevitably I was fired
when a customer breezed past the pay window not paying,
even though my cash drawer didn't come up short.

The last battle was over unemployment.

I alone sat across from store manager, training manager,
2 shift managers and a company attorney.
What they didn't know is that I had just won
a custody case for my son, this was a walk in Baldwin Park.
I used the company's own policies against them
(about customer's not paying) I pointed to their write-ups
shoddy, scratched out dates, the many inconsistencies.

The arbiter listened and the faces across from me
became redder than palm trees on a fry boat.

I collected every fucking penny of my unemployment.

Andrew Romanelli resides in Las Vegas, Nevada where he
was born and raised. He is a teaching artist and IWW
member. His first poetry collection Rotgut (Zeitgeist Press)
was published in 2022, followed by two poetry chapbooks
Supermarket Poems (2023) and One More Night (2025). You
can find him at www.andrewromanelli.com

WHEN YOU FIND OUT

When you find out your dad sold faulty parts
and you tell him that they were faulty, he
tells you he knew they were, and when you then
tell him that people died as a result
of using faulty parts he sold them, he
asks you *What can I do about it?, if
they're dead they're dead,* what can you do about
it? Post the truth on placards? Go on talk
shows? Get the guy indicted for war crimes?
Change your last name, drop his? All the above?

Or when your family pharmaceutical
company pushes opioids and more
folks die than in all foreign wars combined...?
Or when your family company sells beef
from beeves that eat feces for fodder, folks
eat it, and you confront the family Board
and all they do is listen, smile and shrug...?

If any of these dark scenarios
applies to you, you are American.
And if you are not bothered by them, you
are really really an American.

There is another way, however. There
must be or we are damned. So let us try
to find this other way, and let's call it
The Future, or, The American Way.

James B. Nicola is the author of eight collections
of poetry, the latest three being Fires of Heaven:
Poems of Faith and Sense, Turns & Twists, and
Natural Tendencies. His nonfiction book Playing
the Audience: The Practical Actor's Guide to Live
Performance won a Choice magazine award. A
graduate of Yale, he has received a Dana Literary
Award, two Willow Review awards, Storyteller's
People's Choice award, one Best of Net, one
Rhysling, and eleven Pushcart nominations – for
which he feels stunned and grateful.

WHAT DIANE SAID TO ME ON MY FIRST DAY

The job of ocean freight forwarder seemed easy enough
I was supposed to call people after people called people who called
people who I called after people called me after I called them to see if
they got my fax so they could call people who could call the people
who moved the cargo and some data entry

cupcake interview arranged by my future sister-in-law and I was in
a big boy in the big city job
fresh off the SEPTA train in a new shirt
as freshly pressed as my college diploma
and ready to do some serious business

a less than container load of lubricating oil to Dubai here
surfactants to Singapore there and some
magnesium medal power that explodes if it gets wet
all sailing the ocean blue

I called the people who called the people who called the people who
called the people who told the people to move the thing

lunchtime walks past the Liberty Bell
it was easy enough
except when it wasn't

then we all started yelling

the dot-matrix printer jammed hourly
I told the dispatcher Elizabeth when I meant Marcus Hook
and this was all before I knew
a forwarder's spelling mistake once killed a guy in Baltimore

And on my first day
I dropped a bill of lading off at Diane's cubical and the office
matriarch with the homemade retirement countdown calendar
puts down the phone when she sees me approach:
Hey, you the new guy?
puts her hand over the receiver before I can answer:
*Listen, do yourself a favor and get the hell out of this business before
you're too old to do something with your life, okay?*

MATTHEW USSIA

THEY'RE CALLED THE MILL RATS

a baseball team name
coined by foremen and owners
because our grandfathers
would scatter when the whistle blew
at the end of every shift
because they were too proud
to accept voluntary unpaid overtime
at a job where you could die any minute

supposed to be a nod
to the area's rich industrial history
sign of postindustrial resilience
in a town full of modern ruins
poisoned water & chronic abandonment
not to mention the layoffs and Pinkertons
American dreams that lay rotting
reclaimed for friendly family fun
in the land of the terminally bright-sided

Matthew Ussia is director of Duquesne University's First Year Writing Program in spite of the fact that he got a C- in freshman writing and was rejected from Duquesne's MA program. He is also an editor, podcaster, post-doom thereminist, softcore punk, postpunk backup singer, social media burnout, and sentient organic matter. His first book, The Red Glass Cat, was published by Alien Buddha Press in 2021. His writings have appeared in Mister Rogers and Philosophy, Future Humans in Fiction and Film, North of Oxford, MadSwirl, Trailer  Park Quarterly, Anti-Heroin Chic, and Pittsburgh Quarterly among others. More information can be found at www.matthewussia.com.

WE AREN'T REVOLUTIONARIES

*"I don't want to speak too disparagingly on my Generation
(Actually) I do, We had a chance to change The World but opted for The
Home Shopping Network instead."*

~ *Stephen King*

I

Somewhere...
at the crossroads of America
jammed into the orifice of
society and solitude
we were living in
Huxley's nightmare
and Orwell's daydream
constricted by man-made horrors
comprehended daily.

Commodities bought and sold
by our parents who traded
our futures for security.
capitalistic caravans
I can't seem to understand
run rampantly
breaking our benevolence.

Machines made of macerate
the solemn youth
our faith in masters
We disgrace.
We are ageless.
We are eternal.
But, We Aren't Revolutionaries.

II

Back on the beat
my cigarette is lit
the song of these sore feet
bounces off the concrete.
wandering wayward on the wayside
never went so well.

Things are changing;
I can feel it.

Somewhere...
on the Bayshore.

the anthem of
another damaged generation

Rolls the airwaves
of a rock station.
even though the venues
keep closing their doors.

Our pariah of poetics
is giving academics headaches.
touring the great expanse
in vagabond extravagance.

Poet outlaws draw words
from the wind
even though we don't know
if anyone is reading anymore.

We all forgot to laugh
until the jesters
started dropping the jokes.
This Is A New Kind Of Anarchy.

III

Somewhere...
at the crossroads
of America.
art takes shape
in once empty space;
in every dive bar, roadhouse,
coffee shop, bookstore and basement.
the music hasn't died, Mclean!

But, the song is not the same...

Laughter lingers over youthful loons.
music marinates the minds of the masses.
the poem Is changing.
now living and breathing
in every essence
of its own existence.

As long as language is alive
and we make communion
on this broken bread
it will never die!

To the solemn youth
to the faith in masters
We disagree
We are ageless
We are eternal
We Aren't Revolutionaries.

But, This Is A Revolution!

Alex Ragsdale is a New Jersey turned Johnstown, Pennsylvania based poet, musician, and event organizer. Host of Flood City Fables and the organizer of the Bardstock Poetry Festival in Johnstown, PA, as well as a poet organizer with the New Jersey Poetry Renaissance.

EMIGRE

for Hilário and Sergio

The last thing he remembered
was eating sea turtle eggs on the coast
washing each one
down with an iced cold beer.

The mortar peeling from his mind
revealing a tiled heart; the elephant ears
in someone else's garden listening.

He never roamed. He missed home.
Stuck cleaning desks made of glass
with a plastic spray bottle.

In Oaxaca the girls glistened.

The mountains outside Pasadena
reminded him of his father's nose,
that day they fought – his edema,

his fist reaching for the head
of lettuce the snake hid under
moments before his death,

the way he rose,

the way he kicked.

STEVE LAPINSKY

AMBASSADOR BRIDGE

I remember one January,
heading to Windsor –
to meet my girlfriend's family.

Her father abhorred tardiness – she said
he saw it as a class distinction.

I was from Inkster, my father a plumber.
She implored me to bring a bottle of wine.

My tires were bald and there was ice on the bridge.

A jackknifed fuel tanker spread across three lanes.
First responders crawled all over its frame
like Norwegians dismantling a great shark.

The doors of the cab lifted, the man extracted.
I put my car in neutral to keep her alive.
The sky was the color of gasoline,
and the earth hissed like the beginning.

Strangers talked outside their vehicles,
as an overweight police officer redirected traffic.

Her father thought I was a real dead-ender.
and as the cars piled-up behind me
I realized he was right,
pulled an illegal U-turn
and headed back to Detroit.

Steve Lapinsky's work has appeared in magazines such as The Gettysburg Review, Mid-American Review, Gris-Gris and, most recently, CalibanOnline. He teaches at Florida A&M University.

2025 REFLECTIONS UPON THE POEM OF KARIM WAFA-AL HUSSAINI

It's true, I s'pose, we are disturbing their peace if

inequality depends

upon the peace and

comfort of oppressors

Susanne Lorraine Harford (ne Johnston/Bell) is an old Australian-born firm believer in the mysterious, though great, powers of solidarity and love.

THE UNIVERSITY OF REALITY SHOWS

All the years my brother worked
for companies both large and small
and now in his semi-retirement
he finds himself in retail. He's there
because he loves to talk about tools
in the aisles of Lowe's, dispensing
magical wisdom about blade sharpening,
and sandpaper grits, and the horsepower
of routers. His supervisor is twenty-five
years old and nobody knows
how she rose to that position.
My brother cracks wise that she likely
studied at the university of reality shows,
the ones where a single winner is left
standing after sabotaging everyone else's
chances. My brother gets on her
shit list for that remark. I tell him
he's about to experience a brand new
feeling — that one where you sense
hostile idiots are making the decisions
dedicated to complicating your life.
Sure enough, six weeks later he is
let go on some minor infraction.
This is the way it is done. The blame is
laid at your feet. You are told you've
brought it on yourself. You shrug
and accept the pain of having to enter
a market of throwaway labor
where there is always another begging
fool more desperate and compliant.

Tim Kahl is the author of six books of poems, most recently Omnishambles (Bald Trickster, 2019), California Sijo (Bald Trickster, 2022) and Drips, Spills, Bursts, Tangles, and Washes (Cold River Press, 2024). He is also an editor of Clade Song [www.cladesong.com]. He builds flutes, plays them and plays guitars, ukuleles, charangos and cavaquinhos as well. He currently teaches at California State University, Sacramento, where he sings lieder while walking on campus between classes. [soundcloud.com/tnklbnny] [www.timkahl.com]

THE BEATIFICATION
OF FATHER STANLY
"FRANCISCO" ROTHER

The death squad snuck into the rectory past midnight and at gun point demanded of the church keeper to take them to the priest and they put two bullets into Rother who died fighting, helping the poor of Santiago Atitlan, and by the time the first rooster sang, the body lay on the bloody floor. Sometimes all it takes is for someone to label you a communist. Ask Julius and Ethel Rosenburg. Bad words sting the mouth, dull the tongue. The reward for martyrdom is to have your heart ripped out, pickled in a jar and enshrined in the church. The rest is dust and detritus. A crow flies in through the window and pecks at the glass. Motes dance in the rays of light. The meek and destitute clasp their hands expecting nothing short of a miracle.

GentriFried Cumbia

The fixer uppers arrived off Long Beach Blvd and took jackhammers
and paint and turned houses into profit, all along paying Mexicans
peanuts for their labor. Always squeeze and plunder, so it goes where
the hookers walked in for quick blows or handjobs and asked what
kind of music they were fucking to. Mighty buck cumbias and
Norteñas, how money exchanges hands in this sunny land of palm
trees and tall fences. The singed lawns missed the rain. One by one the
houses got modernized and painted, changed hands to these white
young couples who moved down from Silicon Valley. Wanting to raise a
new generation of gringos. They never go away even when they know
this land is not theirs. No matter, they take and take, fix and move the
old folks out who can no longer afford the new taxes. Everyone now
sings this heartbreak cumbia. You can hear it blasting out the broken
windows of the next house. The kids play in the dirt. The old woman
with the umbrella says, "there goes the neighborhood!" Ajua!

Virgil Suárez was born in Havana,
Cuba, in 1962. At the age of twelve
he arrived in the United States. He
received an MFA from Louisiana
State University in 1987. He is the
author of ten collections of poetry,
most recently 90 MILES:
SELECTED AND NEW and THE
PAINTED BUNTING'S LAST MOLT,
published by the University of
Pittsburgh Press. His work has
appeared in a multitude of
magazines and journals in the United States and internationally. He is the
recipient of a National Endowment for The Arts Grant and a Florida Arts Grant.
He lives with his wife and co-editor, Delia Poey, and they make their home in
fucked up Florida. His most recent book is AMERIKAN CHERNOBYL, art, poems,
and photographs, available from Amazon.com.

WE, THE PEOPLE, EIGHTY-SIX 47

I refuse to accept state sanctioned hatred.
I refuse to accept that hatred is considered normal.
I stand against masked agents who rip
The fabric of our nation and the bonds of our unity.
I resist efforts to create agony and distrust.
I stand against those who threaten freedom,
Freedom to speak out. Freedom to listen,
Who threaten us with their detention centers,
Who whisk innocent people away in unmarked vehicles,
Because of the color of their skin or for what they believe.
I resist the masked gestapo and the orange face oligarchy
Who are driven by their fear of the other
And their hatred for everything that makes
America what it is.
When government restricts the rights of the People
We must abolish it.
Resistance is our only option.
Impeach buttercup

Burl E. Battersby is a poet who lives on the shores of the
Salish Sea, in Tacoma, Washington. His poems are usually
pastoral and mostly describe the four square blocks
between South K Street and Yakima near his home. In this
poem he explores his disdain for an orange-faced fascist
oligarchy.

WE ARE NOT MACHINES

The powerful have made us believe
we are small and replaceable
like the double AA batteries
in a remote.

They pit one town against
another, one state against
another to feed their insatiable
capitalist lust.

They treat decisions as if
workers are machines only
secured to a place by
bolts and easily disassembled,

Moved to another factory
to run just as efficiently.
Mercenaries love soulless
things. Management,

With its taste for amnesia,
is like the Wizard of Oz,
hiding their humanity behind
big desks, offices, and rhetoric.

Labor laws and negotiations
prove, ownership will try
to cut every corner and are
hailed by their communication

Departments as savvy businessmen.
They want to treat us at best as
machines, but prefer indentured
servitude. They demean

Our simple hopes and
desires that do not square
with a second home near the ocean
or eating at the hottest restaurant

In town. They want to close their books,
While complaining about taxes to strike
a deal which will defund our dreams.
They know knowledge weakens

Their cause, and bullies are afraid

of strength. They want us to believe
they are broke. They want us to
remain in the dark about sales

Only to shift their goals to suit them,
as if they want us to just shut up
and dribble. They say we are
a family. The logo wear proves it,

Although we are no more than
whatever is mass produced –
our children are nameless, and
we are cursed when we call out

sick, names usually reserved when
something crashes or a machine
needs repair. Long before they would
pity us, we strangely pity them.

We are filled with compassion for the risk,
and for numbers that pollute their minds
as they miss their children's piano recitals
and ball games in exchange for

The score of a spreadsheet as if they are
the ones who carry the real burden
of getting shit done. We bear the brunt
of their failures,

While never sharing in the trappings
beyond pizza or Christmas parties,
as they take home the real money
and eye the next position.

Our raises only mirror inflation,
always explained as business pressure,
but never as a poor business plan.
They will blame us for their problems,

A truly dysfunctional family, but
never the marketers, engineers,
or management. They will call
us lazy while posting record profits.

The dangled carrot is half eaten.
Only fascist laws will stop the march
towards us receiving what should have
been ours long ago. Pizza. T-shirts,
and our fair share of success. Dignity.

If You Can

Month after month, one worker after another
posts a handwritten note on the bulletin board.
Usually, it starts with "Please, if you can" or
"We are taking a collection" for _____ who has
fallen on hard times. But we all know this just
means "life" when you don't have enough money
or accrued time to pay for a sickness or mistake.
They gather groceries, scented candles, and
a few dollars until it becomes the miracle of loaves
and fishes. It's not because they've read the bible
or even go to church, but understand by experience
and decency that the difference between being
the giver and the receiver is the grace of God.
Just when the weight of capitalism is about to break
them, they rescue one another with kindness
that ownership can't be bothered with as they plan
vacations with their wives they don't want to take.

Tom Lagasse has spent the last five years working in a factory. His poetry has recently appeared in numerous publications and anthologies. He was a 2024 Artist in Residence at the Edwin Way Teale House at Trail Wood. He has received recognition for his poetry by the National Baseball Poetry Festival and was recently awarded the 2025 E. Ethelbert Miller Prize. He is the Poet Laureate of Bristol, CT.

FOR ALL THE MOTHERS' TEARS

For all those unseen
hiding beneath the rubble
whose children are double amputees,
just statistics for the war machine

For all those who can't speak,
who've been silenced and shut out
from the national debate

For all those made homeless
by the bombs of indifference,
targeted by sniper and settlement,
the red ink in the ledgers
of a blood-for-profit regime

For all the hostages
lingering in black sites and prison cells
held without charge or trial
hidden away from the spotlight

For all those being starved
and left hungry, those guilty
of being born, of being a thorn
in the side of Democracy

For all those who've ever
picked up a rock
or spray painted graffiti
who've lifted up their voices
and their middle fingers
to the capitalist patriarchy

For all those who've decolonized
their brains and stood
on the right side of history

This poem is for you.

A Message from the Founder of AntiFa

(In the voice of The Joker)

Hello!

Welcome to the show.

As the founder of Antifa
there are one or two things
I would like to say...

First off, fuck Batman...

That's right, he's a spoiled little billionaire
and everybody knows it.

Oh boo-hoo your mommy and daddy got shot ...
Whaa ... mine were never there in the first place
and look at me, I turned out just fine.

No, no, no, no, no...

If you want to fight crime
look in the mirror buddy
how many homeless people does it take
to create one billionaire,
or what are we talking about now
trillionaires coming around the pike soon
well, here's an idea that may just be
a little over the moon for you...
how about pay some damn taxes
or better yet, how about total debt forgiveness
burn the whole damn capitalist system down
I mean with all the money you spend
to be a bag full of dicks
you could end poverty world-wide
billionaires shouldn't even exit
Go Orcas!

Oh, but I'm the bad guy
because one little CEO gets killed
Luigi, that bag full of Monopoly money
was the coup de grace, my friend.

You gotta appreciate the way another cat struts

... but let's get back to business,
cos the Fa's are in Portland now
and I hear they're coming to Gotham next
so we gotta make a plan

... and as the brains of this operation
I'm gonna lay it out for ya

oh, and while we're on the topic
can anyone tell me what the Fa
yes, that's what I said
What the Fa is, in Antifa
Yes, yes, you sir...
what's your name
we'll call you Charlie,
you look like a Charlie,
So, Charlie can you tell us
What the Fa in Antifa
actually means?

YES!!!

You got it on the first try
well done, Charlie
it means "Fascist."

So now, work with me here
if the Fa in Antifa means Fascist
then, if you are anti-antifa
What exactly does that make you?

That's right!

It makes you a Fascist.

So, now that we got that straightened out
let's talk about what we're going to do about it
cos, believe you me, they're coming

... and I was talking to my good friend Kermit the other night
and he said to me,

"I once knew a frog who said,
Instead of leaping over one another
to get what we want
why don't we consider
to take each other's hands
and stand side by side,
and leap together instead,"

Then, he turned to me
with this sparkle in his eye
neigh, what I might say
was this spark of genius,
and said to me in a whisper,
"Follow the frog."

And I was like, "Wow!
What the fuck does that mean?"

... but that was all he said,
and as I'm stewing over this
it comes on me like an epiphany

"Follow the frog...
(boom-chiggy-boom, boom-chiggy-boom)

... Follow the frog...
(boom-chiggy-boom, boom-chiggy-boom),"

Fascists are immune to everything... except mockery
and their henchmen don't know how to deal with
being made to look like a bunch of cowards and fools
... which they are, by the way...
let's make no mistake about that...
now in the good old days
it'd be all Molotov's and slashed tires
why, isn't anyone ice-picking their tires
... just kidding...
but really, does anyone want to talk
about freeing these hostages?

And while where on the subject
Fuck Israel and Free Palestine
What you let happen to Gaza they'll do to us here too.

So, this is just a little reminder
to all of you who say Fascism is coming
... baby, it's already here.

The only question left is,
"What are you going to do about it?"

Oh... and the second thing I wanted to say...

Fuck Trump.

Mark Lipman, US National Beat Poet Laureate (2024-2025); founder of the press Vagabond and the Vagabond Poetry Caravan; the Culver City Book Festival, and the Elba Poetry Festival; winner of the 2015 Joe Hill Labor Poetry Award; the 2016 International Latino Book Award and the 2023 L'Alloro di Dante; a writer, poet, multi-media artist, activist and author of fifteen books, began his career as the writer-in residence at the world famous Shakespeare and Company in Paris, France (2002-2003). He worked closely with such legendary poets as Lawrence Ferlinghetti and Jack Hirschman, and for the last twenty years has established a strong international following as a leading voice of his generation. His radio program, Poetry from Around the World, aired from 2023-2025 on KPFK 90.7FM Los Angeles, and he's the host of the poetry adventure television series, Endless Horizons, with HC Media in Massachusetts. As Mark continues to travel the world, he uses poetry to connect communities to the greater social justice issues, while building consciousness through the spoken word.

INDEX OF ARTWORK

VAGABOND